FACING THE MUSIC

FACING THE MUSIC

AND LIVING TO TALK ABOUT IT

NICK CARTER

DEDICATION

This book is dedicated to all of the broken individuals and families in the world—all of the people who have suffered from neglect or abuse, who have inflicted pain on themselves or on others, who have been compromised by drugs and/or alcohol, who have lost their lives or lost loved ones to those substances, or who know and care about someone who has experienced these things. To those of you who are seeking help, and to those who aren't even aware yet that you need help—including members of my own family—I'm responding to your S.O.S. even if you don't think you've issued one, because I've been where you are now and know that change is possible with the right help. It's my sincerest hope that you will find a path back to physical, emotional and spiritual health and that this book will be a real help to you in this way.

Wishing you all the best this life has to offer,
Nick

NOTE TO READERS

As with all books, this one contains opinions and ideas of the author. It is intended to provide helpful and informative material on the subjects addressed in the publication. It is sold with the understanding that the author and publisher are not engaged in rendering medical, health, psychological or any other kind of personal professional services or therapy in the book. The opinions, ideas and concepts in this book are not intended to diagnose, treat, cure, or prevent any medical, health, mental, or psychological problem or condition, nor are they meant to substitute for any type of professional advice. The reader should consult his or her medical, health, psychological or other competent professional before adopting any of the concepts in this book or drawing inferences from it. The content of this book, by its very nature, is general, whereas each reader's situation is unique. Therefore, as with all books of this nature, the purpose is to provide general information rather than address individual situations, which books by their very nature cannot do.

The author and publisher specifically disclaim all responsibility for any liability, loss, or risk, personal or otherwise, which is incurred as a consequence, directly or indirectly, of the use and application of any of the contents of this book.

CONTENTS

FOREWORD... 1

INTRODUCTION 3

Chapter One: FOR LESLIE AND FOR YOU 11

Chapter Two: PAST MATTERS.......................... 31

Chapter Three: MY BSB FAMILY 53

Chapter Four: DRIVING BLIND 75

Chapter Five: THE NIGHT OF THE ZOMBIES 101

Chapter Six: COOL SPRINGS REHAB 117

Chapter Seven: THE HOUSE OF CARTERS COLLAPSES . 137

Chapter Eight: HEART SICK 157

Chapter Nine: THE COMEBACK 175

Chapter Ten: THE DAY-TO-DAY CHALLENGES
            & REWARDS............................. 193

DISCOGRAPHY & AWARDS 219

NOTE FROM LAUREN............................... 223

ACKNOWLEDGEMENTS 225

BIBLIOGRAPHY 227

RESOURCES 231

FOREWORD

I'VE KNOWN NICK Carter for more than half his life. In that time, he's always been like a little brother to me.

We first met when I was 19 and he was only 12. Kevin Richardson, the oldest member of Backstreet Boys, was 21. Given the age difference between Nick and the rest of us, it just seemed natural to take him under my wing. I'd give him tips on how to navigate the group dynamics or advice on relationships and life in general. Now it's really great to see that he's the one dropping knowledge.

I've always had compassion for Nick. He's gone through a lot in his lifetime—and so much of it has been played out in public. Growing up can be intense under any circumstance, but it is especially so in this crazy business. I was glad to have been his ear then and I'm still glad to be there for him today. As we've grown older, we've definitely grown more reflective. A while back we even started to read self-help books, looking for answers to our individual challenges in life. (Yes, celebrities definitely have those, too.) One of the great things about our friendship is that we've not only applied what we've learned from those books to our own lives, but we've also shared valuable information from them with each other. Nick has combined the best advice he's ever read or heard with his own personal experience and self-discovery and has written the kind of book I'd recommend to anyone.

I'm not sure, during the crazier days of our career, any of us would have predicted that Nick would write a book like this, but that's what's so remarkable about him. He never had the benefit of a normal education— he had to earn his high school degree on the road—and yet Nick proves that life, with all its ups and downs and twists and turns, can be our best teacher. There's a lot of wisdom in what he has to say that you just don't learn in school.

One of the things I've always admired about Nick is the way he dives head first into a project. He's a real go-getter and has lots of enthusiasm for whatever he's involved in, but he has this free and easy-going way about him, too. His philosophy is "it's all good". He basically just wants to see everybody be happy and live the best life they can. This book reflects those traits; it provides some great ways to help people be proactive, improve the quality of their life, and attain the kind of peace we all strive for. And while it's honest about how hard that can be at times, it's optimistic too. Nick has examined his own heart and mind. He's worked really hard to get control over his life, his choices, his weight, and his overall health. He's even gone the extra mile by doing research into the newest information for maintaining good health.

Nick has always loved to brainstorm. Like him, I think ideas are great, though not so much if you don't follow through. What makes me really proud of Nick right now is that he did follow through on some of his best ideas ever—from his commitment to taking charge of his own life, to sharing how he did it with others so they could follow his lead. This book is proof that he's a man of his word. He really is the perfect person to show others how they can overcome their own obstacles because he's done it himself and because he still strives to be better everyday.

It's really awesome to see Nick come into his own skin. He's matured so much in recent years, especially in how he deals with his anger. Rather than throwing fists, he's found power in using his words. He's found a new calm. His example continues to inspire me in so many ways, and I know it will inspire others, too.

This book is for anyone who thinks that no one out there has problems as bad as theirs; it's for anyone who needs to be reassured that with a strong dose of will-power and determination there is always a way forward; and it's for anyone who needs encouragement—regardless of whether they've been a leader or follower before—to be their own leader now. The past is the past, but the present, and how it will impact the future, is yours to decide today.

—Howie Dorough

INTRODUCTION

WHILE WRITING THIS book I took a break to get together with some old friends and a few million other people. That's when I found myself standing on a stage in New York City's famed Central Park kicking off the Labor Day weekend. I was performing in public for the first time in many years with all of the original members of Backstreet Boys. This was the launch of our 20th anniversary reunion tour and it was being broadcast around the world as part of the television show *Good Morning America*.

It was surreal to be up there with Brian, Howie, A.J. and especially with the band's prodigal son and returning member Kevin. I was overwhelmed by the experience and just stunned at the response of the audience. A crowd numbering in the tens of thousands packed into the park as far as I could see and they were singing along to every song, cheering, and having a great time. Honestly, I couldn't believe *that* many people still loved our music.

All of the guys in the band were caught up in the emotion of that moment, too. Believe me, we've each had ups and downs over the years so we don't take anything for granted at this point in our lives. As the group's youngest member, I was definitely the least mature and the least prepared to become a pop star. Looking back, it truly scares me to think how many times I came close to blowing all the great things that being a member of BSB brought my way.

Standing on stage in Central Park on that beautiful day, I was so grateful that I hadn't become a casualty of my own recklessness—that I hadn't killed myself while doing drugs, driving drunk, or hanging with self-destructive people. I was also grateful to be performing well, feeling healthy and full of life again. Grateful, too, that I could enjoy the moment with a clear head—not drugged, drunk, or hung-over—and that I was capable of having an intelligent conversation with our television hosts. Finally, I was grateful that I'd come such a long way in how I felt about myself.

...DRUGS AND ALCOHOL...
NEARLY KILLED ME.

Knowing what I'd overcome in the past, and feeling capable and worthy of a great future made that day in New York City all the sweeter. During the darker times in my life I never would have imagined a day like that could happen. What I try to remember now is that we never know what is possible for us in our lives. We may tend to focus on the worst-case scenarios when we're feeling down, but I'm here to tell you, the best-case scenarios can happen, too. Still, you will never enjoy the best life has to offer until you decide that you deserve it and until you go after it with everything you've got.

I nearly checked out several times before I accepted that I was worthy of a better life and then committed myself to pursuing it. If I hadn't finally taken responsibility for my own happiness, I easily could have missed out on BSB's 20th anniversary—or worse, missed out on the rest of my life. There is no more direct way to say it: mixing drugs and alcohol and engaging in other self-destructive behavior nearly killed me.

My beautiful sister Leslie battled many of the same demons as me and, tragically, she didn't make it. In many ways her death was the catalyst for this book. I've written it in Leslie's memory, though I sincerely wish I could have given it to her before she died. It's filled with answers to the kinds of questions I've had about my own choices and it has lots of sound advice and guidance I've picked up from professionals who really know how to help people like me overcome our toughest challenges.

I can't shake the feeling that Leslie would have found some truth, hope, and direction in it . . . and that it might have helped save her life.

Now, I am not saying I have all the answers to other people's problems or even to my own. You don't need to look very hard for proof that I'm not a perfect person. Between the tabloid reports of my arrest for DUI, the crash and burn interviews I've given about my "night of the zombies," my family's disastrous reality show *House of Carters*, and the life-threatening heart problems I've developed due to my hard-partying lifestyle, my flaws and mistakes are pretty well known.

Yes, my life has been blessed in many ways, but it's also been a train wreck at times. I have not been a very good example in the past, and I still struggle each and every day to do better and to be better.

So, I haven't written this book because I think I'm some kind of shining example. I'm still a mess at times. But right now I'm a mess on the mend. And I'm on the mend partly because I learned from other people's experiences and coaching. Writing this book is a major step in my continued process of healing, but it is also a way of "paying it forward." I couldn't help Leslie in time, but maybe all that I know now could help others avoid the same mistakes in life that I've made.

There are many ideas, theories and practices that have helped me get my act together and I am determined to share them here with you. I didn't invent this stuff, by the way. I'm not claiming to be Dr. Phil or Dr. Oz or Dr. Ruth either. Most of the guidance and advice offered in this book has been around for a long time. You may already be familiar with many of these methods, but maybe you thought they wouldn't work for you or your particular situation. I'm hoping you will give them a try anyway. Take it from me; it's worth the effort. I've probably been right where you are at one time or another, so I know these tools can help.

There is no one quick cure, unfortunately. If there were, I'd be lined up at the pharmacy for a prescription. I'm painfully aware, also, that you can't expect to change lifelong behavioral patterns and dump your worst baggage overnight. I sure haven't.

That brings up another point. I've tried to be honest in these pages. I've shared feelings and thoughts I've rarely talked about in interviews. I detail my experiences with rehab and Alcoholics Anonymous programs, and I also write about going to a therapist; something I still do regularly. You may be one of those people who think that's a rich guy's thing, or something only weak and needy people do. Think what you want, but just know that I didn't grow up as a spoiled rich kid. I'm actually from a blue-collar Tampa neighborhood and one thing I've learned is that rich or poor, all people can benefit from professional help, just as I have.

Although friends had suggested I try therapy for several years during my worst times, I fought it. Like most guys, I believed I could handle my own problems. I was wrong. I didn't have a clue. Take my word for it, when you become deeply dependent on alcohol and drugs, the chances are slim to none that you can get out of it on your own. If I can convince just one person who needs help to get it from a professional, I'll consider this book a huge success. That's how important it is.

I didn't really understand how therapy works at first. But I soon learned that a therapist is just someone trained to help you figure things out for yourself. They give you tools that you otherwise wouldn't have. Some therapists are expensive, but you would be surprised how many are affordable. Some even provide their services for free or at very low cost because they work in programs funded by schools, companies, churches or communities. Many clergy members and school counselors are trained in therapy, so you might want to check them out first. Certain insurance policies only require a $10-or-$20 co-pay when seeing a therapist. If you don't have insurance, look for a training clinic or community health center near you; they often work on a sliding scale based on what you can afford. Joining a support group can help, too, as those are often free and run by mental health professionals. And of course, read self-help books—lots of them. What you find there can be indispensable.

It's true that not everyone needs therapy, but I think most people could benefit from it in some way. Before I went to therapy, I tried handling my emotional problems by self-medicating with alcohol and drugs. I think we all agree, that's not a long-term solution. There is no shame in asking for professional help. In fact, it's a very brave and smart thing to do. This is especially true if you have an addiction or if you are unable to pull yourself out of a depression, and, even more so, if you have thoughts of harming yourself or others. I cannot stress this enough; help is available. Reach out for it. If you don't know where to look ask a friend, a family member or anyone else you trust. And if you don't trust anyone you know, look for a mental health hotline to call. They can help you before you end up beyond help.

Throughout my odyssey, I've learned that we all have the power to change our lives for the better, and that change begins the minute you decide you deserve the best life you can create. You can begin by identifying the negative influences and experiences in your past and doing all that you can to move forward without them. Claiming a better future means building on your talents and gifts, learning from your mistakes, dealing with your demons, and following a plan that is flexible and includes both short and long-term goals. There will be distractions and disruptions along the way, but if you focus on your goals, you will be taking active control of your own mental, physical and emotional well-being. And before long you will be surprised at the amazing opportunities that come your way.

My hope and belief is that one day you, too, will feel the joy and gratitude that comes with taking responsibility for your own happiness and that you, too, will reap rewards the way I felt I had on that awesome summer day in Central Park.

You do have to seriously *want* to be happy, though.

I know, I know—anyone who's hit rock bottom, or is well on the way to doing so, has got to be asking, *"Why wouldn't I want a better life?"* But it's not as silly a statement as it sounds. The truth is that even when we absolutely hate the way things are going, we may not really want to change because we've grown used to being unhappy and miserable and we're afraid or just too lazy to make the effort. We tend to sit on our *buts,* as in:

- *But what if I leave this abusive person and can't find any one else?*
- *But what if I quit my lousy job . . .who will hire me then?*
- *But what if I can't deal with life once I'm off drugs or have stopped drinking?*
- *But what if I'm just not cut out for success?*

Sometimes, we find it easier to stay where we are even when our lives suck. It can be very tempting to play the victim, blame others for our problems, or hold pity parties for ourselves, but none of those strategies will help to make life any better. To do that, you have to learn to **kick your buts.**

Don't be surprised if it's not easy. I wasted a lot of time and opportunities playing the blame game, and trying to drink and drug my way through life. Some people hit bottom and never get up, while others rise from the wreckage and build something much better. I managed to crash and burn a couple of times before getting serious about making the changes I needed to make.

Even now, I seem to take a step back for every couple of steps forward, but I haven't bottomed out in a while and I take that as a really good sign. A lot of great things are happening in my life, including the revival of the Backstreet Boys and the deepening of a romantic relationship that has lasted longer and has meant more to me than any others. So, I have hope for even better days ahead.

In this book, I'll be offering ten basic concepts that have helped me get to where I am now. Really, these are just common sense things that you probably know already, but it's amazing what can happen when you actually put them to use. I'll offer examples of what each of them has done for me, and I will share tips and observations that will help you see why this stuff can help you get out of whatever rut or bad situation you are in and on track to change your life for the better.

Here's a quick outline of what's ahead as I share my own story and as we embark on what I hope will be a successful journey together, because as much personal growth as I've had, I'm still a work in progress too.

No. 1: *DECIDE YOU DESERVE THE BEST*
Make the decision that you are worthy of happiness and fulfillment and that only you are responsible for your own life.

No. 2: *LET GO OF YOUR PAST & RISE TO YOUR FUTURE*
Acknowledge where you've been and then focus on where you want to go.

No. 3: *GO WITH YOUR STRENGTHS*
Build your life around your talents and interests.

No. 4: *LEARN FROM YOUR MISTAKES*
Deal with setbacks and see failure as a learning experience.

No. 5: *DEAL WITH YOUR DEMONS*
Overcome fears and insecurities.

No. 6: *DEVELOP A PLAN AND ACT UPON IT*
Create a step-by-step plan for achieving short and long-term goals based on principles and values.

No. 7: *FOCUS ON CONTROLLING WHAT IS WITHIN YOUR CONTROL AND LET GO OF THE REST*
Be proactive not reactive, making adjustments as you go.

No. 8: *TAKE CARE OF YOUR MIND, BODY & SPIRIT*
Pay attention to the mental, physical and spiritual elements of good health.

No. 9: *PREPARE FOR OPPORTUNITIES AND EMBRACE THEM*
Keep preparing and growing so you are ready to jump on opportunities, even in hard times.

No. 10: *PRACTICE FORGIVENESS & GRATITUDE EACH STEP OF THE WAY*
Forgive yourself and others and express gratitude daily to stay on track.

Remember that to get where you want to be, you will have to face the realities of where you are now and then do whatever hard work is necessary to lead you forward. If you do all of that, it will have been well worth the effort. In addition to a promising future you will have the added benefit of knowing that you deserve all the good things coming your way because you truly earned them.

CHAPTER ONE

FOR LESLIE AND FOR YOU

THE HEADLINE IN the *New York Daily News* reporting my sister's death told only a small part of her story:

NICK AND AARON CARTER'S SISTER LESLIE DIED FROM DRUG OVERDOSE, WAS UNDER THE INFLUENCE OF SEVERAL PRESCRIPTION DRUGS: POLICE REPORT

The 25-year-old singer had moved to family's home in upstate New York to kick habit

Leslie died on January 31, 2012 in Mayville, New York where she was visiting our father. She left behind her 10-month-old daughter Alyssa and her husband Mike along with the rest of our family. It's difficult for me to even write about her death. I doubt that the grief and the hurt I feel will ever leave me. I've always wanted the best for my family. I love all my siblings, and though our relationships have been complicated, I've tried to help each of them many times. I've given them money and other material things, but I realize now the best thing I could have done for any of them was to give them this book.

The greatest *gift* you and I will ever receive is the realization that we can and should take responsibility for our own lives. We can rise above anything that has happened to us because we have the power to choose how we respond to those events. We should never waste time waiting for someone else to make us happy when we have that ability ourselves.

After my own long struggle in which I sometimes played the victim and blamed others for my challenges, I've discovered there is nothing more fulfilling and rewarding than stepping up and doing whatever it takes to claim the life you want.

UNLOADING BAGGAGE

My siblings and I grew up in an unconventional family. We were not dealt the greatest cards when it came to our home environment. Maybe you weren't either. I know we all have baggage we carry around with us. For a long time, I let what happened in my past spoil my vision of the future. I didn't think I deserved success or love or happiness. In some ways, I was hanging on to a victim mentality, playing the blame game, feeling sorry for myself. You know how that worked out for me—not well.

But once I dumped that kind of thinking and decided that I wanted and deserved something better, I went after it. I stopped waiting for things to change and I actively made changes of my own. Although I've made a lot of progress, I'm still working on myself. I'm not entirely where I want to be yet, but every day that I take a step in the right direction is a good day. I know there are great things to come.

What we all have to bear in mind is that you and I were not put on this earth to suffer and struggle. We are all here to make a contribution. We may have some work to do, but just acknowledging that we aren't the individuals we want to be yet is a major leap toward making things better. The key is to stay focused and committed to moving forward every day.

That's not to say you won't take a few backwards steps now and then. It happens. Believe me, I know. Just understand that you have the power to choose a better life for yourself. Once you make that choice, there are many people willing to help you and many ways you can help yourself, too.

I've worked hard to find healthier ways to think and to live. I've learned a great deal about how to deal with my demons. Professional therapists have helped me understand what has made me insecure and self-destructive at times. Yet, I'm still prone to messing up. Perfection is a great goal, but I'm not there yet. I'm often guilty of not following the advice of others, including my therapist, fellow Backstreet Boys, and friends who've reached out.

I still struggle with my issues, including insecurities and a lack of trust. Many of my challenges are related to the way I grew up. That's not an excuse. Lots of people have grown up in dysfunctional families. Some have survived serious abuse. Many have lost their parents or other loved ones. The point is that there is no such thing as the perfect life. Most people have had bad things happen in their lives, yet they've managed to deal with them by recognizing it's not what happens to you that shapes your life; it's how you respond to it. And it's not where you come from either; it's where you end up that counts. The example of these people should give us all hope.

PERCEPTION VERSUS REALITY

Before you can heal, however, you have to understand where the hurt comes from. In the case of us Carters, it comes from a very particular kind of family dysfunction. Members of our family have a tendency to do and say things without thinking first.

I'm as guilty of this as anyone. I've blown up in anger or frustration and later realized I never should have let those words out of my mouth because words do hurt. I've had to work on thinking before I act. It's all about being aware of the thoughts and feelings that affect you, then taking just a split second to consider why they are there and how to respond to them wisely. If you don't pause and take stock of those feelings, whatever you do next will only come back to bite you in the ass.

For most of my life, I *didn't* evaluate my thoughts or emotions. I just reacted by lashing out. Then I learned about the concept of filters.

Each of us has unique ways of looking at the world based on our experiences, both good and bad. If you grew up in a loving and supportive home where you were encouraged to develop your mind and your talents, the way you look at things is likely to be much different than the way someone who has been abused or neglected looks at things. Past hurts, rejections, and failures can wear you down. They can make you distrustful, wary, and unwilling to put yourself out there for fear of experiencing those horrible feelings again. The first step toward changing your life is to change your filter. That means deciding that no matter what happened to you in the past, you still deserve the best of what life has to offer.

THE FIRST STEP TOWARD CHANGING YOUR LIFE IS TO
CHANGE YOUR FILTER.

I know from experience that working hard and achieving your dreams won't bring true happiness and fulfillment unless you believe in your heart that you are worthy of it. So, before any changes can be made successfully, we have to examine who we are now and who we want to be going forward. Admittedly, it's not an easy thing to do. Looking deep inside of yourself isn't fun. It takes a mature person to conduct an honest appraisal of character, attitudes, prejudices, judgment, and other critical aspects of personality. To help yourself feel worthy of success, you need to understand the experiences and influences that have contributed to the particular life filter you have in place now.

WALLED OFF

To be blunt, Leslie's and my filters were established when we were very young and they became more damaged as we grew. My siblings and I weren't particularly well-nurtured as kids. I write more about that in the chapters to come, but for now just know that while I'm sure our parents loved us, they didn't demonstrate their love in ways that typically make kids feel safe and secure. We all know that to be loved is one of the greatest human needs. If we don't feel well cared for early in life, it definitely messes with our perceptions and influences all of our future relationships. We may feel we can't trust others. We may drive people away intentionally or build walls around our feelings so we can't be hurt. We may even choose to harm ourselves before anyone else can.

Although the media said drugs for schizophrenia, bipolar disorder, and anxiety were found near Leslie's body, I don't know that she was ever truly diagnosed with any of those problems. Sadly, I'm aware that Leslie had been self-medicating—probably against her own hurt and isolation—for a long time.

She passed away because she allegedly took too many pills, though to this day, I'm not sure how many pills were involved. Her death may have been accidental for all I know. I'm also uncertain if a medical professional prescribed the drugs she was taking. What I can tell you, though, is that whenever I saw her in recent years, she was acting in ways that both concerned and scared me because I cared about her.

During those last years of her life, Leslie was not the person I had known and loved for so long. The lifestyle she was living and the choices she was making when it came to her health had really changed her. She felt she wasn't in control, and I worried about that same thing. One night during a Christmas holiday, she went out partying. When she came home, she told me she thought she should be admitted to a mental institution. She said she'd done things that night that she badly regretted.

My family quickly mobilized and did some research, looking for a place that could help her, but when we told Leslie what we'd found, she'd changed her mind. She thought that she might be better off if she moved to Canada. She actually would've preferred to live with our grandparents in upstate New York, but they feared it would be too hard for them to care for her.

Although we continued to worry about my sister, she refused all of our further efforts to help her. Instead, she asked for money. Unfortunately, I was afraid she'd just use it to buy more drugs. This is such a serious issue today, throughout the nation and around the world. There are so many people in need of professional help who are self-medicating. The misuse of drugs is epidemic. People feel a pill can fix everything. And too often, they think more and more pills will make them feel even better when, in fact, taking more than the prescribed dose can kill you or mess you up for life. It pains me to think that if Leslie had been guided properly, she might still be with us.

A professional therapist, psychiatrist, or doctor won't put you on medication unless you truly need it. And you should never take more than the prescribed dose—or worse, act as your own doctor and self-medicate. I know this because I've had serious issues with alcohol and other drugs in the past, which I certainly regret.

After everything I have been through, and certainly after Leslie's death, I don't advise anyone to do drugs of any kind. In fact, I'm a strong believer in holistic alternatives to traditional medicine because too many traditional medications have dangerous side effects. I like the fact that holistic medicine is intended to treat the mind, body, and spirit as one. It incorporates natural diet and herbal remedies, nutritional supplements, fitness workouts, breathing exercises, acupuncture, massage, and various relaxation methods to help people achieve lasting health.

Once I focused on trying to stay clean and taking better care of myself, I offered to help Leslie do the same, but she wouldn't hear of it. Her walls were up. It's sad, but we were not on good terms when she died. I hadn't seen her for nearly a year before then and can't say that we had much of a close relationship since we were kids. In some ways this is understandable. I am six years older than Leslie, and I joined Backstreet Boys when she was only six. I was out of the house for most of Leslie's childhood. Because we didn't really grow up together, we never had a chance to be as connected as most brothers and sisters.

I do recall Leslie and I having fun though when we were very young, and I prefer to think of those years when she is on my mind. Memories of those times came flooding back to me when I recently watched a home movie made just before I joined BSB. We were living in Tampa then. As a kid I dreamed of becoming a film director some day. I loved making movies with my brother and sisters as actors. I taped a bunch of these home movies after winning a video camera in a competition sponsored by *The New Original Amateur Hour* television show at Universal Studios in Orlando.

In this particular video, I created my own version of a local-news broadcast. Leslie, who was just about seven at the time, was the news anchor. It was touching but sad to watch. She was so young and innocent then. Life's challenges hadn't affected her yet, and her potential seemed limitless. We were just kids playing at home, and the video captured a sweet moment in our lives. Those moments were all too rare.

Watching those home movies made me wish we'd had more of those peaceful childhood memories. Maybe Leslie and I would have been closer to each other and to our other siblings if I'd been around more. I tried many years later to get close to her, but it was difficult to get through the barriers she'd put up by then. I wish I'd done more to break through those barriers before it was too late. I hope she's forgiven me. I've certainly forgiven her.

REACHING OUT

Despite not being there for most of Leslie's formative years, we were both raised under the same conditions in the same incredibly chaotic household. My nickname, Kaos, and the name of my company, Kaotic, are drawn from the fact that our house was so crazy. Leslie was the middle child, which is usually a good position for being sheltered. She did get some protection—mostly from my grandparents who may have spoiled her in their efforts to give her what she so badly needed—but Leslie wasn't entirely shielded. She was just a year and a half old when Aaron and Angel were born. As twins, they attracted a lot of attention. Leslie often said she didn't get as much love as they did. She didn't always handle it well either, and sometimes her actions created friction with the rest of us.

I don't want to defame my late sister in any way, but she was often difficult to get along with. She once went on Twitter and railed against me, telling my fans that I had refused to support her financially after I actually had done a lot to help her in that regard. I was really hurt by that.

It was common for my family members, including my parents, to ask me for financial help after Backstreet Boys took off and we had so much success. I didn't mind at first. I was glad to be able to help them in any way that I could, until around the time I turned 27 and I purposely stopped because giving them money didn't appear to be helping them at all.

I was in the studio one day when I got a call from my sister Angel. She told me to look on Twitter because Leslie was saying bad stuff about me. I was shocked at first and then, of course, I felt betrayed because for so many years I tried to help her. I could only hang my head in sadness after all those things she was saying. She was making public so many personal and private matters that it caused even more of a strain on our relationship. She tweeted that I didn't care about our family any more and claimed I wouldn't help her get a place to live, which was so untrue. If only she could have remembered all the things I had done for her. I'm afraid she was really trying to replace something inside of her that had been lost long ago.

But I couldn't replace what Leslie was missing, or maybe never had. I cared deeply about her and my other family members, but I felt that giving them money only made them dependent on me. I wanted them to be independent and to have their own careers doing whatever they loved. I thought they deserved that joy. Every time I handed them money, things only got worse.

When I stopped supporting family members, they tended to blame me for their problems. Leslie would still call and ask for money even after that. I helped her with a car, and when she wanted to get married, needed a passport or decided to become a citizen of Canada, I helped her find an attorney to handle the details. After a while, I felt Leslie was beyond my reach. Because she continued to abuse drugs and alcohol when I was trying to cut back, I was afraid to be around her. I was worried about her, but I honestly didn't know how to protect her. About three years before she died, Leslie came to one of my concerts in Canada. She was in bad shape. I hadn't seen her in a long time, but she definitely seemed *medicated* then.

I felt uncomfortable and helpless. I was embarrassed to a degree, and I felt guilty too. I thought, *Man, it's my fault she's like this!* I took on the guilt and responsibility for her drug problem because I'd set a bad example. I was in the celebrity spotlight and my brother and sisters were watching me. They saw me drinking and getting arrested for fighting and for drunken driving. I just wasn't a good example for them to follow for a long time.

MISSED OPPORTUNITIES

After I left home and joined BSB, I had a chance to change the course of my life. Many things were better, but instead of leaving the personal chaos behind, I took it with me. I could have stopped what was already a growing pattern of self-destructive behaviors, but I didn't. The other kids in my family looked up to me and when they saw me partying and getting into trouble, they figured that's how they should act too. I didn't take my responsibility as their role model seriously enough. Those thoughts all hit me when my little sister came to my concert in Toronto in such bad shape. She was slurring and falling down. I could not understand what she was saying. I felt helpless and frustrated.

The memory of that is still vivid. Those scenes played in my mind whenever Leslie would get in trouble or do something hurtful. I felt she was reaching out to me with one hand but pushing me away with the other. She wanted money and love, but at the same time she lashed out at me. I wasn't equipped to handle it.

I TOOK ON THE GUILT AND RESPONSIBILITY FOR HER DRUG PROBLEM BECAUSE I'D SET A BAD EXAMPLE.

About a year before she died, Leslie showed up at my getaway home in rural Tennessee. I was in Los Angeles at the time. My security company called and said the alarm had gone off. Leslie had somehow found a way in. I had no idea she was there. Another time, she came out to L.A. and I heard she was trying to find sources for Xanax. I told her to stop, but she let me know, in no uncertain terms, that it was none of my business.

Leslie was breaking my heart. It makes me sad to see my brother and sisters get into bad situations because I think they deserve better. I just wish they felt the same way. One of the biggest behavioral patterns I have noticed in my family is that we often feel we deserve to be punished or mistreated. We tend to be martyrs and victims. This pattern has existed in me and caused me to be reckless with my money and my health and well-being. In fact, behavioral patterns like these can be passed down in families from generation to generation unless they are recognized and broken. I became aware of our family's *victim* pattern during therapy, where I learned that if you don't work to break it, you could pass it on to your children.

My brother and sisters and I all have dealt with the feeling that we are unworthy, and so when bad things happen to us, we feel as if we deserve those things. After I recognized that pattern in myself, I was able to see it clearly in them, too. I tried to help by telling them they had the right to dream big and to be whatever they wanted to be.

Leslie did give it a try at times. She had some success as a singer early on, but she became discouraged when her singing career came to a sudden halt. She'd signed a recording deal in 1999, when she was about 13 years old. She cut an album, but her label, DreamWorks Records, didn't release it right away. They first released a single, "Like Wow!" to build interest. That single made the Billboard Hot 100 and appeared on the *Shrek* soundtrack. One critic reviewed a promotional copy of the album and gave it a very good write-up in *The Village Voice*, but the label canceled its release at the last minute. Rumors spread that Leslie had developed a weight problem that worried the label's marketing people. My sister was really hurt by all the talk about her body.

I FELT SHE WAS REACHING OUT TO ME WITH ONE HAND BUT PUSHING ME AWAY WITH THE OTHER.

She moved to Canada and toured as a singer there for a while. She also did a showcase in New York City in 2006, hoping to get another record deal. For a couple of years Leslie also sang with a band, but they never signed with a label either. It's so tough to make it as a singer. I encouraged Leslie to focus on writing songs because she was really good at that. She had journals full of lyrics. The problem was that Leslie had gotten a taste of what it was like to be a celebrity performer and that became her dream. She wanted to be famous, but songwriters are rarely household names. Leslie convinced herself that fame was the key to happiness, which is a common mistake many young people caught up in the whole celebrity fantasy world make.

Again, it is sort of a family curse. We all seem to want to be famous, yet we don't feel worthy of fame. I guess that's why chaos is such a part of our story. In the days before Leslie's death, our father tried to help her, but his attentions weren't enough. She was broken and none of us could seem to fix her.

People have asked why I didn't intervene and send her to rehab, but for rehab to work you have to be ready to heal yourself. I've been around people who've gone through the process but because they weren't ready to change their lives, the therapy didn't have much effect. Some of them have gone three or four times. What you must realize is that until people *want* to help themselves, nothing will *cure* them. They have to have a real desire to get better; otherwise they'll fall back into their old behaviors as soon as they get out.

Those in need of help have to decide that taking pills, doing drugs, or drinking too much is self-destructive, and they also have to decide that self-destruction is *not* what they want. That's important. But it doesn't stop there. They not only have to want to save themselves, they have to feel worthy of being saved, and worthy of leading a better life once they are saved.

I remember even when we were enjoying our first waves of success as the Backstreet Boys, I was struggling with the sense that I didn't deserve all of the good things that were coming my way. I was not comfortable with all of the media attention or the public's expectation that I serve as a positive role model.

Despite my success with BSB, I was still carrying the burden of insecurity from my past. My therapists would later tell me that a lot of the negative things I did were subconscious efforts to sabotage my career because, as I said at the very start of this chapter, I didn't think I deserved success or happiness. As much as I wanted to help Leslie and my other siblings overcome their problems, I was wary of getting in too deep with them because I had my own challenges. My therapist warned me about this. It's not selfish to protect yourself when you are vulnerable. It's actually very necessary.

Before a passenger plane leaves the gate, the flight attendants instruct those on board that if the oxygen supply is cut off in the cabin, each individual needs to first put their own drop-down masks on before trying to help anyone else around them. You can't help other people if you are gasping for breath yourself. Lifeguards are taught this concept in their training as well. They are instructed in specific self-defense techniques used in water rescue. The goal is to keep the panicking person from drowning the lifeguard who is trying to help them.

We all want to help others who are struggling in their lives, especially if they are our loved ones, but as these universal survival methods prove, you have to save yourself first. Being a martyr or a victim does no one any good. *You* need to be strong, stable, and secure before you can see anyone else to safety.

FEELING WORTHY

I don't share these stories about Leslie's and my relationship lightly. They are not very flattering, but I'm in a much better place now than I was then and feel that I can throw a lifeline out to others. Don't feel badly if you aren't there yet. It's a day-by-day process. Some days I'm much more successful at feeling strong, stable, and secure than on other days. I have many years of bad behavior and negative thinking to overcome. My default behavioral patterns—the ways I act when I don't consciously think things through—are so badly flawed. Believe me, it is difficult to change lifelong patterns. I've needed help from professionals, and there is no shame in that. There is shame only in wasting your life by not making the most of your talents and your gifts and the precious time you're given.

You deserve to feel and look great and to enjoy the best life has to offer. And you must expect those things for yourself. Now that doesn't mean you need to have money or fame to be happy and fulfilled. There have been all kinds of studies showing that once you have enough for life's essentials—food, clothing, and shelter—amassing more and more money doesn't increase your level of happiness. I mean, how many miserable and screwed up rich and famous people have you heard about?

Look at me. I've made tons of money thanks to BSB and I've had my share of fame, but you can't imagine how often I wished I had a more *normal* life, especially in my younger days when I was often lonely and missed my family. I'm grateful for all of the success I've had, but I've also come to understand that real happiness isn't about how many nice things you can buy. It's about finding what you love to do and doing it in ways that make a difference to those around you. For most people, happiness comes from relating in positive ways to the world.

Think about it, what makes you truly happy? (And don't say *shopping!*) Most people are happiest when they are engaged in doing what they love to do. Sometimes they call this being *in the zone* or *in the flow* or *bliss*. For me, it's being on stage performing for an audience, but you can experience the same sense of fulfillment whether you are a number cruncher, an auto mechanic, a house painter, or a dog trainer—as long as that's what you love to do.

WE ALL SEEM TO WANT TO BE FAMOUS, YET WE DON'T FEEL WORTHY OF FAME.

We all have the ability to move mountains and do things that are out of this world if we just use our minds. You can't remain stuck somewhere unless you give up. You don't have to settle for less than what you want to be. You don't have to stay where you are right now. You may not necessarily achieve your greatest dreams, but why not try? What have you got to lose? You know that *nothing* better will happen if you just sit on your butt all day complaining and playing the victim.

I cannot emphasize this enough: You have to believe you deserve the best. You have to want it. You have to go after it. And you have to be willing to ask for help when you need it. I tried to help my sister. I know I wasn't the greatest role model, but I wanted her to be happy and my intentions were good. I wished with all my heart that she would've let me help her, but she didn't and that's just a damned tragedy.

Don't let your talents or your life go to waste. Claim the best life you can imagine. If you need to make a change, do it. When I finally began going to a therapist after acknowledging that I needed help, one of the first things I learned is that all these filters I had in place since childhood were not just affecting my thinking and the way I perceived the world, but they were also affecting my ability to communicate with the people I cared most about.

I WISHED I HAD A MORE
NORMAL LIFE

My relationship with my brother and sisters was toxic in many ways. We weren't good for each other even though, deep down, we love each other. This is all very, very sad to write about and sadder to have experienced. I still grieve over Leslie's death and the fact that she died before we could come together on good terms.

DON'T LIVE WITH REGRET

It breaks my heart to even think about it now, but I did not go to Leslie's funeral. I was in New York City when she died. I couldn't get on the plane and go up there because some members of my family were blaming me for her death. It hurt me so badly to hear them say things like that. It really stung me.

Some were saying that if I'd been there for her, she wouldn't have died. That's the most horrific thing someone could say. At one time, I might have allowed them to do that to me, but by the time Leslie passed away, I had become much more secure and healthy; I knew better than to accept that lie as truth. All I've done is love my family while trying to protect myself.

I did intend to go to Leslie's funeral. I wanted to see my sister for a last time. I wanted to say goodbye to her that day, yet I also knew I had an obligation to take care of myself, and there was a fine line between those two choices. I had promised to be there and I needed the closure, but when I spoke with the family members organizing the services and they unloaded on me like that, I just knew I couldn't be there.

I got sick talking to them. I was crying, lying on the floor in the bathroom for two hours. I was so upset; I couldn't go up there to our mother's place because I didn't want to be around all that negativity.

My body and my mind couldn't have taken it. I used to allow negativity to overwhelm me, but I can't physically do it anymore. I have to take care of myself. I have to protect myself from situations that might send me back into that black hole of depression again.

I struggle every day with the emotional aspects of losing my sister to drugs and alcohol. It's a daily battle for me to stay away from them myself. Leslie knew that I loved her just as I love everyone in our family. They are my blood, but loving someone doesn't mean you have to take abuse from them. Being there for family is important in most cases, but if the situation is unhealthy and could hurt you emotionally or physically then you need to protect yourself. I've had to learn the hard way to recognize which situations are not good for me.

I USED TO ALLOW NEGATIVITY TO OVERWHELM ME, BUT I CAN'T PHYSICALLY DO IT ANYMORE.

I thought Leslie and I were making some progress on our relationship before she died. I loved her and I know she loved me, despite our differences. It is a horrible feeling to lose a loved one in any situation, and even worse to lose an important person in your life with hard feelings still lingering. I've made peace with my memories of Leslie now, but it took a long time.

I would encourage you to never be put in the same position. Don't let disagreements or feuds keep you apart from those you love. Forgive them and ask their forgiveness because you never know when they might be gone forever.

RISE ABOVE

Leslie never learned that we can rise above our circumstances. We can change our lives by changing our attitudes and the ways in which we respond to things that happen to us. I can't tell you for certain what was going on in her mind when she took the pills that they say killed her. But I know that Leslie never fully grasped something that changed my life—and could possibly change yours too.

When I was a boy living in a dysfunctional family, I couldn't control my circumstances. The fighting and drinking were inescapable. As I grew older, I did finally get away; I escaped physically by leaving the house and emotionally by abusing drugs and alcohol. I was punishing myself for something I had no control over. Eventually, I found a better way—a way I will describe for you in this book.

YOU SHOULD NEVER LIVE WITH A VICTIM'S MENTALITY

Understand for now that when you find yourself in a bad situation, you should know that what happens to you does not define you. By that I mean you can rise above a bad environment, a hurtful relationship, or anything else beyond your control that happens to you. What matters is how you respond. You have full ownership over your choices. You can make a decision, as I did eventually, to take charge and move on in a positive direction. You may not see a way out now, but there is a way. Do not give up. Do not punish yourself like I did for too long, or sadly, like Leslie did.

You should never live with a victim's mentality. You may have been abused, but that does not mean you deserved it. No one deserves abuse. You should never allow others to hurt you physically or mentally. You can walk away. There are safe places for you to go, better places where you can command your daily life and never again be a victim. It is torture and torment to live that way.

I wish Leslie and I could have healed our relationship. I wish she'd accepted my offer to join me as I worked to become healthier. I wished the timing had been better and that I had committed many of my healing experiences to paper sooner. On so many levels, I can't help but think that this book could have made a difference in her life. Although she is gone now, I do take some consolation in knowing that Leslie's death was not without meaning. The loss of my sister inspired me to write this book. It may not have been available to help her, but it is my sincerest hope that it will help other people. Please, let's do this together, to honor the memory of the sister I loved and lost, and to help you claim the best life possible— the life you deserve.

PERSONAL NOTES

CHAPTER TWO

PAST MATTERS

MY FIRST CHILDHOOD home was an apartment above The Yankee Rebel bar in Jamestown, N.Y. Owned by my parents and grandmother, it was the area's most popular bar and disco, and sometimes they had strippers too. My dad was the deejay, bartender, and host. We lived upstairs, so our place was party central after the bar closed. My parents and their friends were big drinkers. I'm not judging them. That's just the way they were when we were growing up.

Going to college and getting an education weren't priorities in my rowdy family. Things like building character and taking care of your mind, body and spirit were rarely discussed around the dinner table. It seemed like there was always a party going on, or a fight.

Family legend has it that when I was two years old I crawled into one of The Yankee Rebel's liquor storage rooms where I was caught drinking for the first time. My parents always laughed at that. I laughed too, for a while, and then I didn't laugh at it any more.

I know now that it's possible to drink responsibly. If you can do that, more power to you. But I didn't see much of that kind of measured behavior growing up. I didn't practice it much either. These days I try to think of alcohol as a drug—one of the biggest and most abused in my opinion. Certainly, that was the case in my family.

We moved to the Tampa, Florida area in 1986 when I was six years old and my sister BJ (Bobby Jean) was two years old. My parents bought the Garden Villa Nursing Home, where they did everything from caring for patients to making the beds, tending the landscape, and cooking the meals. We lived in a little place on the grounds. Leslie was born in the nursing home that first year in Florida, and the twins, Aaron and Angel, arrived about a year and a half later.

By then, we had moved to a house across the street. There was a lot of pressure on me to take care of my younger brother and sisters because my parents worked such long hours. I remember freaking out a little when Aaron and Angel were born. I went into their room the day they came home from the hospital and felt a sudden surge of panic when I saw their little cribs next to each other. My first thought was, "Now I'll have to be in charge of them too!"

I was scared of being left alone with them while my parents were out. I was afraid I wouldn't know what to do, especially if there was a problem. When I described that scene to one of my therapists, he stopped me and said, "You know it was illegal for your parents to leave you at home alone when you were that age, don't you?"

I didn't know that back then, and even if I did, what good would it have done? I just thought it was normal for me to babysit the younger kids while my parents worked. I didn't know any better. My big objective back then was to keep my parents happy so they wouldn't yell at us, spank us, or get into a fight over us. When my dad came home from work each day, I worried about whether he would be upset or happy. Usually, on the days he was happy, he'd been drinking.

Sad to say, some of the best times in our childhood were when my parents drank and partied because at least then they weren't fighting. Of course, sooner or later an argument would start and things would turn ugly.

STRESSED OUT CHILDHOOD

As the oldest, I felt responsible for maintaining everyone's happiness. I guess that's why I'm an entertainer now. Back then, it was all about keeping the peace and not getting into trouble. Really, when I think about those days, we had the most fun when Mom and Dad were at work and it was just us kids at home. My sister Bobbie and I were in charge and we'd come up with all of these great games to play. The bonds forged in those days were strong, and I'm sure they are what still gives us hope that one day we'll all be able to get along better than we do now.

When our parents were gone, we were free to pretend that things were normal. Those times formed the basis of our love for each other. I got to be the big brother to Aaron back then. We spent hours jumping on the trampoline in the backyard, having a blast. I think he looked up to me at the time because I was there for him and we were best friends.

Those times will always remain special in my mind, but I also remember being afraid my parents would come home and find something to upset them. I scrubbed the linoleum floors on my hands and knees until they were shiny because I thought it would make them happy. We all wanted to please them, to win their love and approval, which is normal for kids. I just don't think most kids had to work so hard for it.

...I FELT RESPONSIBLE FOR MAINTAINING EVERYONE'S HAPPINESS.

At night, we'd go to our rooms to get away from the arguing. We could hear things breaking all the time—furniture, glasses, and anything else they could throw. My dad owned a gun and he'd shoot it out the window sometimes when he got really mad. Fear was an everyday part of our household. My dad ruled by intimidation. We never saw physical violence between my parents, but Dad would spank me with a belt in front of the littler kids. I was always the example. He'd pull down my pants and hit me. Dad clearly took out his stress on me. Discipline isn't all bad—kids need rules and boundaries and consequences, but the extent of the discipline Dad doled out on me was wrong.

My parents didn't have college educations. They were blue-collar people and they had to work hard to provide for us. They always stressed about money, which is another reason they turned to alcohol so much. I'm shocked to see home movies taken when I was nine and ten; in them, I'm pretending to be drinking. Clearly I'm mimicking my parents.

In one home movie my cousin and I are acting as if we were going out to a bar like two adults. We danced and feigned we were partying. Looking back at how alcohol was part of our playtime, I realize just how deeply my parents' drinking affected me. It was as if I was programmed to drink. Their volatile relationship also negatively affected my perception of how adults should act and what relationships should be like between men and women.

HOUSE DIVIDED

Sadly, our parents didn't hide their battles from us. Mom and Dad often brought their fights into my bedroom or BJ's because we were the two eldest. They would say, "We're getting a divorce, which one of us do you want to live with?" This happened many times over the years. BJ and I would tell them that we'd go with either one just to get it over.

The threat of divorce was always present in our home. We lived with it constantly. My oldest sister and I had to adapt to our parents holding a breakup over us until it got to a point where we actually hoped it would happen. Privately, we'd think: *Just get divorced already.*

My therapist says it's no wonder I have commitment issues. I was 23 years old by the time my mom finally filed for a divorce. My dad came to me and asked what he should do. I said, "You need to break up with her." It shouldn't have been my responsibility to tell him that. They both asked the younger kids the same thing and it affected them badly. A parent is supposed to lead by example, and teach and guide their children. They shouldn't have put that sort of responsibility on their kids.

SADLY, OUR PARENTS DIDN'T HIDE THEIR BATTLES FROM US.

We all felt that my parents were bad for each other. Their drinking and fighting never subsided, even when money was much less of an issue. During the divorce battle, they fought over who would have custody of Aaron. My little brother made his first record at the age of ten, and by the time the divorce proceedings had begun, he'd already earned millions from albums and concert tours. Aaron was only 15 years old when he filed a petition for legal emancipation because of the way our mother was managing his earnings.

During their fallout, he made public comments about our mother stealing $100,000 from him. Then shortly after that, he withdrew the petition. I don't know exactly what happened in Aaron's case, but I eventually hired professionals to manage my career so I would never find myself in the same position.

The turmoil and drama just never seemed to end with my family. Havoc ruled most of the time, and we all paid a price for it. Because most of us couldn't handle it very well, it ultimately drove us apart.

You could make a strong case that I had fewer reasons for turning to drugs and drinking than anyone else in my family. My career with the Backstreet Boys and the financial rewards that came with it should have given me enough fulfillment and motivation to stay straight. I should have focused more on my work and all of the opportunities that came my way because of it. But instead of going with the good, I couldn't seem to shake the bad.

STOPPING THE NEGATIVE CYCLE

I'm fortunate to be living the dream as far as my career is concerned, but for the longest time I was unhappy because I didn't take the time to examine my feelings, really think about what I hoped to accomplish, or prepare myself for the kind of life I wanted. That's what therapists and psychiatrists mean when they talk about beginning *from the inside out.*

Until you do that, you're bound to just keep repeating the same self-defeating patterns that have made you feel unhappy and stuck in the first place.

So many people repeat self-sabotaging and harmful behavioral patterns like alcoholism, drug use, or physical and sexual abuse without knowing why, until they come to terms with their past and see just how their own patterns mirror those of their parents. In my own search for answers, I've learned that my father came from a household similar to the one he created for us. I loved my Grandpa Carter, who was actually my dad's stepfather. (Dad never knew his real father. I've tried to find out who he was, but so far I haven't succeeded.)

Grandpa Carter mellowed as he got older, but he was abusing alcohol throughout my dad's childhood. He fought with my grandmother because of his drinking and, as a result, Dad saw lots of drunken violence as a boy. My dad was also disciplined in the old fashioned way, which may explain why he took the belt to me.

Like my father, I repeated many of the same patterns. Drinking, drugs and anger led to embarrassing incidents and even to arrests for fighting and drunk driving that I'll write about later. Things really got out of control when I began doing cocaine so I could stay awake and keep partying longer. I became that guy staggering around the club at the end of the night as the lights switched on and the deejay played the last song. (For some reason it always seemed to be "Don't Stop Believing," which is ironic, because Journey was our family's favorite band.)

OUR HOUSE WAS WILD.

Too often on those crazy nights, people would recognize me, and I'd be ashamed to be seen so gacked up. I was a serious mess there for a while—drunk, stoned, high on coke, overweight and mindless. Eventually, I realized that heavy drinking and drug use was endangering my career and causing serious health problems, but before then, it seemed as if I was hell-bent on destruction.

I began drinking heavily in my teens and then moved to drugs at eighteen or nineteen, starting with marijuana and moving up to cocaine, Ecstasy, and prescription painkillers among other substances. Its defenders say that pot is not a gateway drug, but for me and for many of those I know, marijuana definitely led to other drugs. Mine is not an unusual story; in fact, it's all too common.

The real gateway to alcohol and drug abuse, though, was my childhood and the environment my parents created for my brother, sisters and me. I'm not saying I'm a victim of bad parenting or that it's an excuse for my own mistakes, but it does help explain a lot of my behavior.

My parents have their good points. My mother especially was very encouraging and supportive of my singing career. I love both of them. I just wish there had been more emphasis on education and character-building and less on drinking and partying when my siblings and I were growing up. I also wish there hadn't been so much arguing, fighting, and yelling. There was just way too much drama and not enough nurturing in our lives.

Our house was wild. My entire family tends to think that normal communication involves screaming at each other. Conflict resolution was never in our vocabulary. We tended to fight like pit bulls, make up with floods of tears and bear hugs, and then within a short time, set back to fighting again, repeating the cycle over and over.

SKELETONS IN THE CLOSET

Everyone has skeletons in the closet, things they've done and regretted or things that happened to them that they are ashamed to talk about. You and I have to accept the fact that we are human and we make mistakes, and that there are times when we can't control what happens to us. We don't choose our families or the tragedies that occur in our lives.

Like the old country song says, "Sometimes you're the windshield and sometimes you're the bug." We get blindsided at times, and other times we sabotage ourselves. That's part of life, part of being human. There is freedom in accepting that, just as there is freedom in forgiving those who've hurt you and also in forgiving yourself for making mistakes. Now that doesn't mean we can just do whatever hurtful things we want and then make it right by forgiving ourselves. We have to take responsibility, and then try to do better.

Several years ago, I realized that all my issues and skeletons were piling up to the point where they were like huge stones in a backpack I was carrying around with me all the time. They were weighing me down so much that I could hardly make a move. You can't believe what a relief it was to talk through those issues with someone who was supportive and encouraging and who had very practical ways for dealing with them in a positive manner.

I am not a professional therapist and it is not possible for me to sit down with you and guide you one-on-one through the process that helped me. What I can do, however, is encourage you to find someone you trust, someone with experience in counseling and therapy, or at least a very good friend or a nurturing family member to help ease your burden.

I fought the idea of going to therapy for a long time. It seemed like something for messed up people, or for someone with more money than sense. Like many folks, I was not willing to admit that I couldn't handle my own problems. I had the attitude that *I'm good. No help needed here. I've got it under control.*

Except, I didn't.

The truth is that a therapist doesn't handle your problems for you. Instead, therapists give you tools so that you can help yourself. They have training, experience and a much wider and deeper perspective than most people, and they are skilled listeners. Mostly, my therapists just let me talk. Part of me still fights the idea that I need professional help, but we all need someone to talk to and the therapists I've had really have helped me see my life more clearly. Friends can be great, but they will often judge you according to their own biases and perspectives. Some might be afraid to tell you what they truly feel. So, I recommend a professional.

I don't believe that the majority of people need drugs to overcome psychological issues, but each person is different. I do know that it's been a great help just getting things off my chest that have bothered me and have festered over time. The stress from carrying around heavy baggage like that can make you physically sick, so that is another reason to look for someone you can trust to listen and offer guidance. I went through that for more than two years while stuck in a negative and unhealthy relationship with a girl. She was jealous of my career success and tried to make me feel guilty about it. I felt trapped, but because of the environment I grew up in, I really didn't know what a healthy relationship should be like.

I was still a teenager, but I actually moved in with this girl and her family for a while, which was like jumping from the frying pan into the fire in some ways. I don't blame the girl. She was young too. We both had insecurities and baggage. My career was taking off so fast neither one of us could keep up with everything going on.

Our relationship became so stressful that I became physically ill. I developed a cough that wouldn't go away and my complexion turned gray. I was afraid there was something seriously wrong with me. That is how powerful the mind and our emotions can be. They were eating at my soul.

I REALLY DIDN'T KNOW WHAT A HEALTHY RELATIONSHIP SHOULD BE LIKE.

If you find yourself in a similar situation, I suggest you seek help because it's tough for you to find a way out on your own. Someone you trust to have your best interests at heart can help you make the hard decisions you'll need to make in order to remedy the situation. Be aware that some of your decisions may come with consequences. Sometimes you might be in an unhealthy relationship or you might be in an environment that is not good for you and you'll not only have to recognize the situation for what it is, but you'll have to change things about those relationships. If you find yourself too upset, stressed out or feeling sick over it, as I did, you may need help from a therapist to figure out what to do.

When I finally got out of the relationship that was troubling me so much, the feeling of freedom and liberation I felt was fantastic. I had no idea just how much that situation was affecting me. I still needed help from a therapist to resolve the issues and baggage I carried into the relationship, which is another important thing to remember. Sometimes the problem isn't the other person, or isn't JUST the other person. Bad relationships can grow worse because of what you bring into them, too.

LOOKING AT YOUR BACK-STORY

One of the mistakes I made, which I hope to help you avoid, is that for the longest time I never stopped to ask why I was being so self-destructive and angry. It never occurred to me to look at where I'd been, where I was headed, and where I wanted to end up in life.

Even when people who cared about me tried to warn me, I mostly blew them off. I didn't want to evaluate my actions or think about *why* I was choosing them over other options. I thought I was in control until I found myself at the bottom of a deep black hole wondering what the heck had happened to me.

It's taken me a long time to climb out of that hole and put my life back on track. One of the first big steps I took was to look at what led me to nearly self-destruct, examine why that happened, and decide to take a healthier and more constructive path.

Once you truly believe that you deserve a better existence, you'll have to clean house of the negatives in your life. By that I mean you have to clear out all of the hurtful and self-defeating baggage that's stacked up over the years so you can start your new life without any old burdens.

Every song, movie plot and book of fiction has a back-story. Many singers, screenwriters, actors and authors consider that history when writing or performing. They ask what has happened to their characters in prior years to make them act the way they do in the song, movie or book. Your back-story may say a lot about you too. So in this chapter, I'm asking you to consider the people, events and circumstances in your life that may have influenced your behavior to this point.

YOUR BACK-STORY MAY SAY A LOT ABOUT YOU TOO.

Some of those people, events and circumstances may have had a positive impact, but if you have struggled like me, odds are that some of them were negative influences. To help you understand how to do this and why it is important, I've shared some of my own back-story with you—things I've never talked about publicly. Now, please think of your own history and those influences big and small that might not have served you well. Think about the influences that have affected your thought and behavioral patterns, especially those that have led to self-destructive or hurtful actions you've come to regret.

When you do these self-destructive and hurtful things, you may find yourself thinking: *That's not like me. I'm not the kind of person who does something like this.*

Thoughts like that are good indications that something has thrown you off. By identifying those negative influences, you can analyze them and then resolve to make changes so you can return to the person you really are or the person you really want to be.

BAGGAGE INSPECTION

Bear in mind, the factors that may have had a negative influence on you could have occurred at any stage in your life, so it might help to make a list of the good and bad things from as far back as you can recall. Before you do that, though, you need to get your mind clear. That means no alcohol or drugs or any substances that cloud your thinking. Once you've cleaned up, whether that takes professional rehab or just self-discipline, then you can take an inventory to see what events and experiences are causing self-destructive behaviors.

Once you've written down the important events and experiences, try to understand how each one affected you. After you've done that, you can begin the healing process.

If you have difficulty taking this inventory, it might help to review your life in blocks of time, including your years in pre-school, grade school, high school, college and your post-graduate years, too. You can also look at the influences of family members, friends, teachers, coaches, bosses, teammates, co-workers, and others who might have had an effect on your thinking.

In general, look for key moments and the most emotional times you can remember. Our actions also can be greatly influenced by tragedies or the loss of a loved one, or by experiencing fear and stress over long periods of time.

You may want to first identify the most damaging and self-destructive behaviors you seem to repeat and then try to trace those back to when you first practiced them or where you first learned them. Remember, you can't move ahead if you are stuck in the same patterns that have blocked your progress so far.

I finally came to the realization a few years ago, with the help of my therapists, that I needed to examine what I'd been through and who I'd become. Call it soul-searching or self-assessment; it's all about increasing your self-awareness, which has been just huge for me.

Self-awareness includes understanding why you do what you do, what triggers your anger, what makes you do self-destructive things, or why you repeat the same unproductive behaviors over and over again.

Have you ever found yourself wondering: *Why did I do that? How could I have said that? What was I thinking?* We've all been there. The goal is to think and reflect *before* you act so that you aren't just acting on impulses without considering the repercussions and consequences of your actions.

Building greater self-awareness can save your life, or your career, or your relationships. Being more aware of the triggers that set you off might just keep you from being the drunk driver who killed some innocent person, or from killing yourself, or hurting someone you love.

NO LONGER A VICTIM

There is another aspect to self-awareness that I've found very helpful: it's actually taken me out of the victim mode that I mentioned earlier. For the longest time, I blamed other people and my past for my problems. I can't tell you how joyful it makes me to stop feeling like a victim and to take responsibility for my own life. A victim has no hope. A victim can't see better days ahead. A victim lets other people or events determine the course of his or her life.

I never want to be the victim again. I am so lucky to be out of that mindset. I broke free of it after finally becoming aware that I had to change some things. I had to accept that I needed help, that what I'd been doing wasn't working. Blaming wasn't working. I needed to get in position to take control. If I hadn't made changes and if I don't stick with them, my life could easily become a tragedy like Leslie's or like so many others who've fallen to drugs, alcohol or despair.

A key point for me came when I asked a few simple but critical questions:

- *Is this really who I am?*

- *How did I get to be this way?*

- *Who do I really want to be?*

- *How do I become that person?*

A VICTIM
CAN'T SEE BETTER
DAYS AHEAD.

You and I can choose the lives we want. Each of us has that power, but we have to act upon it. We can't put it to use if we are caught up in the blame game. Sure, maybe we've had some bad breaks. Maybe you've been abused, or neglected, or have been subjected to violence. Terrible things may have happened to you and I'm sorry for what you've suffered and endured. But remember, whatever has happened to you does not define you. You still have the ability to write your own story. It may not come easy. You may have a lot of work to do. But many, many people have overcome terrible events and gone on to do great things. If you want to have a better life, you have to dedicate yourself to pursuing it. That may mean admitting that you don't have all the answers. You may have to educate yourself, just as you are doing by reading this book, or may have to ask for help.

LIVING THE DREAM

Challenges pop up now and then for all of us—sometimes they even occur daily. There may be times when you feel like troubles are just coming at you one right after the other. One positive way to look at this is to keep in mind that dealing with tough times is part of life. In fact, *it's part of being alive.*

Think about it: The only time you won't have some sort of challenge is when you are dead and buried. As long as we are alive and breathing, we're going to have to deal with bills, sickness, tough jobs, and relationship troubles. Those challenges are just part of life so you might as well accept them, deal with them, and move on.

Stuff happens. The good news is that when bad stuff happens, you have a choice in how you deal with it. You can let it send you into a downward spiral, throwing you into that dreaded black hole of despair, or you can rise to the occasion and handle it in a positive way that may very well lead to the best days you've ever known.

Remember the opening scene I described in the introduction? I was standing on stage in Central Park singing with the reunited Backstreet Boys to kick off our 20th reunion tour. Thousands of people were cheering. The sun was shining. Kevin was with us again. The harmony was back, *LOL*, (no pun intended).

YOU DON'T HAVE TO
GO THROUGH WHAT
I WENT THROUGH.

I wanted to drop to my knees and scream with joy and gratitude. That great moment would never have happened if I had not finally stopped to examine my life and ask myself what was making me put my entire future at risk. It's sad that I had to hit bottom before I asked myself the tough questions and made the changes that were truly necessary in my life. But sometimes you have to learn where the bottom is so you can recognize that you don't want to stay there. Hopefully you will bounce back quicker than I did. I really do believe the best way to learn is through experience, but you should learn in a safe and healthy, non-destructive manner.

You don't have to go through what I went through. And believe me, you don't *want* to.

You may have heard it said that the definition of insanity is doing the same things over and over while expecting different results. If you don't examine your past, acknowledge those things that have held you back, and commit to moving forward, you will very likely find yourself stuck in your own insane cycle of unproductive behavior.

I sure did. I spent most of my teens and twenties sabotaging my career, and my life in general, by self-medicating with drugs and alcohol as a way to deal with my insecurities, anger and fear. Through therapy, the guidance of friends and working to educate myself and make smarter decisions, I began to make some positive changes. I came to realize that instead of running from my past or trying to numb myself to it, I needed to examine and understand it.

I had to look back and really comprehend where I'd been and how certain events and circumstances affected me before I could move forward to where I want to be. It's like planning a trip. If you go to Google Maps on the Internet, you first have to establish where you are before you can map out where you want to go. In this case, though, we're not just talking geography or your physical location. We're also looking at where you have been mentally and emotionally, and maybe even spiritually if you want to go there too.

AN HONEST APPRAISAL

It's important to be very honest here because you are basically looking at what's been wrong with your life so that you can actually make it right. That means telling the truth about your past and acknowledging the bad as well as the good. If you take your car to the repair shop, you don't hide the fact that the engine is leaking oil, or that the brakes are shot. You give your mechanic the list of everything that's wrong so he can fix it. The same holds true when looking at your past. You can't skip over anything that's uncomfortable to deal with because those negative issues are probably the most important to examine and understand.

You can't go back and make things better either. And you certainly can't fix everyone in your life. But you can fix yourself and that should be your focus. You deserve the best life has to offer. You may want to help others and that's a noble concept. First, though, you have to be strong enough yourself.

I tell myself all the time that to help and lead others, I have to serve as a positive example. I'm not always successful, but my goal is to get my act together, keep it together, and inspire others to do the same. I've done it physically, and I'm working on it mentally and emotionally every day. I figure if my brother and sisters and others I care about see that I'm healthier, making better decisions, and am more hopeful and optimistic, they'll want to be the same way. And they'll know if I got my act together, then it must be possible for them to do it too.

TEARING DOWN THE WALLS

For a long time I tried to hide from my problems rather than fix them. One of the things I did was push bad memories back into a corner of my brain where I hoped they would stay locked away. Psychologists and psychiatrists say that repressing memories can sometimes be a good thing, especially in the case of really traumatic events that might overwhelm us or cause us to react in negative ways. But sooner or later, for better or worse, we have to deal with even the most traumatic events because the mind becomes overloaded if we don't. Deep negative memories will surface and sometimes their resurfacing can trigger self-destructive behaviors like self-medicating with drugs or alcohol.

REMEMBER, TO GET BETTER, YOU HAVE TO BE BETTER.

You may need help dealing with repressed memories. Many people do, including me. If you're worried about opening the door to something you can't handle, please find a professional therapist, a counselor, psychologist, psychiatrist, clergy member or at least a good friend or family member whom you trust to be there for you. I'm very glad that I've had professional help sorting through the skeletons in my closet, so I encourage you to find the same.

Once you've acknowledged the past and all of the good and the bad it holds, you should commit to leaving it behind you, adopting healthier behaviors and perspectives, and moving ahead in a more positive direction. This may also require forgiving those who wronged you, and even forgiving yourself for your mistakes or foolish and self-destructive actions.

Remember, to get better, you have to be better. You have to clean up your act if you want to clean up your life. I'm working on that now and I anticipate working on it the rest of my life. I don't expect to achieve perfection, but I'm determined to make it my target so I'll keep striving each day, month and year.

I try not to have regrets because it's important to keep looking ahead, but I know in my heart that there were many years when I could have done more with my life. I've had a lot of opportunities that I didn't make the most of. I wasted way too much time partying, getting drunk and getting high on one drug or another.

I was carrying on a terrible family tradition. I have friends, including some of my fellow BSB members, who grew up in families where the emphasis was on things like faith and education. Honestly, I didn't know those sort of families existed until I met upstanding people like BSB members Brian Littrell and Kevin Richardson.

DON'T BE STUBBORN LIKE ME.

In the pages ahead, I'll tell you more about these two cousins. They are humble guys who'd be the first to assure you that they aren't perfect. They'd probably even say they've made mistakes in life too. I look up to them and admire them because, for the most part, they've built on the strong foundations, principles and values their parents wisely provided them.

RISING ABOVE

While my parents didn't teach me much in the way of values and life principles, I did learn those things from reading books and witnessing the examples of friends like Kevin and Brian. It wasn't until my mid-twenties that I began to see how important it was to have guideposts to live by. I could've avoided a lot of problems and been spared many war wounds if I'd been taught them at a younger age. If you haven't found your own values and principles to live by yet, please learn from my mistakes. Don't be stubborn like me. Set guidelines for yourself. They could very well save your life.

Without them, I became a product of my environment. But at least now, I'm determined not to be a victim of that environment. I am committed to rising above the life I was handed, so I can create the life I want. You can do the same. You have the power to choose how you will spend the rest of your time on this earth.

Are you like me in that you've wasted too much time drinking and doing drugs? If so, you can change all of that by figuring out why those vices seemed like a such good idea in the first place, then deciding you don't believe any of the myths that those bad habits were built on anymore.

Maybe you haven't been motivated to go after your dream job. Or maybe you are in a relationship that hasn't worked out. Think about the last time you were truly happy and excited about your present and your future. What was going on then? How can you get that back? What could you be doing that would fulfill you and make you want to jump out of bed every day? Look within yourself and ask what's kept you from making a change, then look for new and more powerful ways to motivate yourself to take a positive step toward that change. Next, we'll look at one very good way to do that. Once you've figured out what has made you weak and unable to claim the life you want, you'll be ready to identify and build on your strengths.

PERSONAL NOTES

CHAPTER THREE

MY BSB FAMILY

MUSIC WAS A great escape from the chaos at home when I was a kid. I had a small radio with silver knobs and a chrome casing. At night, I listened to rock and R&B stations and somehow the songs made me feel better. One of my favorites was "Bizarre Love Triangle" by New Order. I could tune out my parents' arguments, get lost in a melody and disappear into my own world. Music was a comfort for me even before I realized that I could build my life around it.

MUSIC WAS A GREAT ESCAPE FROM THE CHAOS AT HOME WHEN I WAS A KID.

The stress and lack of nurturing at home took a toll on all the Carter kids. Our schoolwork suffered and we were often in trouble for acting out in class. My sister BJ started as the best student in our family. Because she'd earned straight A's, she was picked for the honored position of student patrol officer. In that role, she would help kids cross the street before and after classes. I was jealous of BJ and the other school patrol members, mostly because they got to wear super cool neon-colored safety belts. As things got worse at home though, BJ became rebellious and her grades dropped.

I, on the other hand, was never much of a student. While the teacher talked, I'd find myself daydreaming. The studies seemed beyond my grasp. I felt lost and very insecure. I was never in the advanced classes with the smartest kids. My classroom was one of those portable units that always seemed reserved for the worst students. I felt like an outcast. It was as if they put us in there so we wouldn't infect the smart kids with our contagious stupidity.

All in all, school wasn't a great experience for me. I was bullied some, especially at the bus stop. The street we lived on in Tampa—131st Avenue—was in a pretty tough neighborhood. One kid terrorized me even though our sisters were friends. He beat up most of the kids who rode our bus, so I guess it wasn't personal. I just tried to stay off his radar or at least out of his reach.

Studying and doing homework were difficult for me, especially when there was so much drama between my warring parents. When Nintendo video games came out, I spent hours playing them. My mother tried to pry me away, but that was pretty hard to do. The one thing we both liked was music so that became something we shared. There was always a radio or stereo on in our house. My parents may have cashed in on the disco era when they owned the tavern but they were mostly big fans of the golden oldies of rock and roll from the sixties and seventies—what my mom called *real music*.

She liked harmonies and strong vocals. In fact, one of her favorite songs when I was little was "Bridge Over Troubled Water" by Simon and Garfunkel. She bought a cassette tape with the song and played it all the time, so I knew it by heart. When I was eight years old, Mom was working in the kitchen one day and she heard me singing that song in the backyard.

I often sang while bouncing on the trampoline, but this time I was on solid ground pretending to be on stage at an outdoor concert. I imagined the blades of grass were my audience. (It was a very *green* crowd.) Mom suspected that I planned this as a performance for her benefit since I was belting out a song she loved, but I was singing for the fun of it.

My parents always said that I was a natural born ham. Mom has written that sometimes she feared I was overly needy and starved for attention. When I think about it, there may be some truth to that as she and dad worked so hard they weren't around very much. If I was hungry for affection and attention, singing that song sure did the trick.

Mom—who genuinely thought of herself as an unbiased observer—immediately decided that I was destined for stardom when she heard me singing that day. She was so impressed, she dragged me into the house to sing for my dad too.

This was the first time my parents realized I might have marketable talent, though Dad was less convinced of my greatness than Mom. He wanted a second opinion, and probably a third.

I INHERITED DAD'S BLUE-COLLAR WORK ETHIC AND DRIVE...

Dad was a total realist about life—not at all what you'd call an optimist. My father was a truck driver before he became a bar owner and nursing-home operator. (He'd met my mom on the road—he picked her up while she was hitchhiking. He charmed her by giving her a ride, but he also warned her never to do it again.)

I inherited Dad's blue-collar work ethic and drive, and I have to say that those gifts have served me well. Still, as hard as my dad and mom worked, they struggled to pay the bills. Money was always an issue. When I first started to develop my performing skills, Dad would blow up over the cost of my singing and dance coaches, and of traveling to auditions, rehearsals and performances. He questioned whether there would ever be a payoff for the investment he and my mom were making. I could hardly blame him. He had other kids and a lot of expenses.

One of the incentives for me to work harder and harder was my desire to make up for those expenses. I really wanted to show my appreciation for the sacrifices and the time my parents put into my training. I also wanted to earn enough money so my parents would never have to fight over finances again. When my singing career took off, I did pay back my parents and I made up for the some of the things my siblings didn't get, too. I even tried to help them out before I was making big money. The first singing competition I won was a talent show on the pier in St. Petersburg.

I was ten years old and there was a crowd of only 20 people, but I won the grand prize of $100. I remember taking the check home to Dad; he was sitting on the couch watching television.

"Hey Dad, look what I did. This is for you. I want you to have it because you work so hard," I said, handing him the check.

He mumbled something, then thanked me. He may have been embarrassed that I was giving him my winnings, which I understand. I didn't mean to make him uncomfortable. My only goal was to provide him and my mother with some peace of mind. My thought at the time was that if I kept giving him money, he and mom would be happier, but it never seemed to work out that way, even when the checks I brought home were for hundreds of thousands and even millions of dollars.

The lesson I ultimately learned from these experiences was that my goal should never be to make more and more money. I realized that once you covered your bills and a few other basic comforts, more money does not bring you more happiness—in fact it often brings more problems, jealousies and greed.

Instead, the thing that makes me truly happy is making the most of my talent for singing and performing. That became, and still is, my career goal.

Ours wasn't exactly the Osmond family or even the Partridge Family, but our family tree did include other musicians. Mom and Dad both played the guitar some and we all sang when we went on vacations or when we were just hanging around the house. I've never had a problem keeping a beat, which may be due to living above The Yankee Rebel when I was a baby and hearing the thumping of disco music through the floorboards all night.

Anyway, it was around the time that teen pop singers and the first boy bands began making waves that I guess Mom decided if Tiffany and Debbie Gibson, New Edition, and the New Kids on the Block could make it, so could I. The next thing I knew, she had me booked for singing lessons, dancing lessons, and every other kind of lesson in the star-making machine. We burned up Interstate 4 between Tampa and Orlando as we hit all the talent competitions and auditions for theme park shows, musicals, dinner-theater, and commercials.

My theatrical career was actually launched shortly after the day Mom witnessed my backyard performance. I was in the fourth grade at Miles Elementary School when the kid who'd been chosen for a leading role as Raoul in the production of *Phantom of the Opera* got cold feet. The teacher in charge of the play, Miss Montes de Oca, had to find a replacement quickly. She'd heard that I was taking singing lessons and auditioning around the area, so she recruited me to step into the part.

...THE THING THAT MAKES ME TRULY HAPPY IS MAKING THE MOST OF MY TALENT FOR SINGING AND PERFORMING.

I definitely wasn't one of the cool kids, an athlete or an honor student before then, so it was sweet to step in and take the role of Raoul, especially since the guy who had chickened out was one of the smartest kids in our school and was on student patrol too.

Being cast in the *Phantom of the Opera* was one of the best things to happen to me at that time. It was one of those rare moments in our family when everyone seemed to join in the fun. Even Dad rallied and got into the spirit. He went to work building the chandelier for the set, which was the centerpiece on stage. Mom worked on the play too, making costumes. They brought the other kids to rehearsals and to the design sessions, and everyone seemed to have a good time without any drinking, fighting or yelling. For a moment there, we felt like one big happy family.

PLAYING TO YOUR STRENGTHS

Even if you never made it past Introduction to Psychology 101, you can see what drew me to performing. All of us Carter kids craved parental attention and affection. Everyone seemed excited about the play and my role as the Phantom. It really brought us all together.

No matter what was happening at home, everything seemed better when I was singing. Instead of the bickering that marked so many of our days and nights, my parents were happy when I sang and so were my audiences. I was happy too. I poured all of my energy into the music because when I performed, my worries, fears, and insecurities disappeared. It was a high like nothing I'd ever experienced, and the larger my audience the better it felt.

There's no doubt that I threw myself into singing, acting and dancing with more enthusiasm than I'd ever shown for schoolwork or sports. My mom dedicated herself to helping me chase my dream. Some have questioned her motives over the years, but I have to credit her with making sure I received the necessary training and for doing all the work required to turn my passion for performing into a career.

MY MOM DEDICATED HERSELF TO HELPING ME CHASE MY DREAM.

She supported me as I progressed through a series of coaches and trainers. At age 10, I found myself beneath the wings of Bob Karl and Sandy DiMarco, professional dancers who owned the Karl & DiMarco School of Theater & Dance in Tampa. One of the first classes I took with them was tap dancing. I was horrible at it. Bob Karl, who looked more like an old-fashioned gangster than a Julliard-trained choreographer, didn't seem to enjoy watching me trip over my own feet either. He was nice about it most of the time, but trying to turn me into a dancer made him grumpy.

In no time at all, I found myself banished to the back row of Bob's class. Once again, I was put with the slow learners. Maybe Bob thought it would help me to watch all the other kids in the front row get the moves right.

I did ultimately improve enough to land a spot as a performer in a troupe that was every straight boy's wildest dream. Bob's wife and co-owner Sandy DiMarco had a side job as the choreographer for the Tampa Bay Buccaneers' halftime shows. Sandy put together a team of beautiful cheerleaders—and me!

Actually, the bikini-wearing, pom-pom swinging Swashbucklers were more like a cross between Victoria's Secret models and the Rockettes. The Bucs were my favorite team, and I was also a big fan of gorgeous, scantily clad young women, so I was a very lucky boy. Don't get me wrong, Backstreet is a great group. Kevin, A.J., Brian, and Howie are my brothers and fun to hang out with, but they don't quite do for me what my first group did. I enjoyed every minute of the Swashbuckler experience, though not nearly as much as I would have enjoyed it if I'd been about ten years older.

This was back when Tampa's NFL team played in the old Houlihan Stadium, which was demolished in 1999. The Buc's creamsicle-colored uniforms from those days are still my favorites, but the teams weren't very good. I guess that's why they needed a big halftime show to prevent the home crowd from just going home. We did our best during every game to keep them in their seats.

Sandy surrounded me with my own special mini-group, calling us Nick and the Angels. Our routine included performing Elvis's "Jail House Rock" and Jerry Lee Lewis's "Great Balls of Fire." My guess is that 99 percent of the guys in the stands who weren't related to me or in my grade school weren't even aware that I was on the field with the Angels and the Swashbucklers most of the time. That didn't bother me though.

I FELT LIKE I WAS PART OF
SOMETHING SPECIAL.

Walking onto that Buc's field for the first time with them was an incredible rush. There were thousands of people cheering every move. It was scary and exhilarating at the same time. Is *scarilarating* a word?

That's when I became truly addicted to the joy of entertaining. It was so exciting. We felt like we were part of the Buc's team and the whole organization. The girls treated me like their favorite little brother. Strangers cheered us. Kids wanted our autographs. I felt like I was part of something special. My parents and brother and sisters were all excited for me too, which made things a little better at home.

Sandy DiMarco sent me to perform with the Angels and Swashbucklers at smaller venues around town, too. Those were mostly appearances to promote the team or community events. Some of us also participated in Showstoppers regional talent competitions against other performers, where we won a lot of contests. I still have those black and blue ribbons with first and second place written on them.

As the only guy on the squad, I tended to stand out. The fans gave me a lot of attention, which boosted my self-confidence and helped me become even more comfortable in front of crowds. Not that stage fright was ever a problem for me. When I heard the applause and cheers from thousands of people, nothing else mattered in that moment.

I loved being on that field, no doubt about it. Still, there was something deeper that drove me to work harder on my singing and performing than I'd ever worked in my life. To put it as simply as I can: *It felt right.* It made me happy. I could spend hours and hours singing and playing the guitar. Even practicing dance routines didn't really seem like work to me.

All the driving and running around and waiting for *cattle-call* auditions could be a drag, but once it was time to perform I forgot all about the hard work that went into preparing for that moment. I just dove in and within the first few notes of a song, I was in my own world. I didn't win every role or every audition, but I felt like I was learning something and getting better. Even the directors, producers or casting agents who chose someone else often had encouraging words for me. They told me I was a quick learner with natural talent, and that I stood out from the crowd. So I quickly got the sense that my mother's enthusiasm wasn't just a *mom thing.*

In some ways I'd found an even larger and more reliable family—my musical family. I felt comfortable and welcome. I felt as if I belonged, as if I spoke the same language as other performers and musicians. Those feelings were strong—so strong that they made the bad things in my life more bearable.

THE GIFT THAT KEEPS ON GIVING

It's still that way for me today. Every time I'm on stage the crowd energizes me. I put out a lot of effort and positive energy, but even more comes back to me. I love to perform, pouring out my feelings and disappearing in the moment, whether I'm singing to a packed stadium or in a small club. I am one of those lucky people who early in life discovered a gift, a talent, and a strength that has served as a foundation for everything else in my life.

In this chapter I want to help you figure out how to generate happiness in the same way, from the inside out. I'm not referring to just a moment of happiness or a few laughs. I'm talking about building a life around whatever gift, talent or strength you have that excites you and makes you feel valued and connected to the world around you.

Once you've accepted that you are worthy of a better life and you have worked to identify and change the harmful behavioral patterns and self-sabotaging thinking that may have held you back in the past, it's time to decide what your strengths are. Like many people, I came from a troubled family without a lot of resources, but after I dedicated myself to a career in music, my life took on incredible momentum. Making it as a singer wasn't as easy as it might have looked from the outside and I have to work every day at staying sharp, but I am so grateful for my career. Music not only saved my life, it gave me a life.

MUSIC NOT ONLY SAVED MY LIFE, IT GAVE ME A LIFE.

Now, what about you? What are your strengths, talents, gifts, and passions? What can you build your life around? There are a few telltale signs to look for if you haven't yet identified a strength. Here are just a few:

1. What are you drawn to time and again? Is there something you want to do during every spare minute?

2. What fills your bucket? Is there some activity that is so rewarding and fulfilling for you that you never get tired of engaging in it; in fact, is it something you'd even do for free just because it makes you happy? (Pretending for a minute, of course, that you didn't have bills to pay or the standard requirements for food, shelter and clothing).

3. What comes easily for you? Is there a school subject, art form, craft, sport, skill or trade that you picked up quickly and then seemed to improve upon every time you do it?

4. What makes you stand out from the crowd? Think of any time when a friend, teacher, coach or classmate has said, "You're really good at this." Or "I wish I could do that as well as you."

BUNDLE OF JOY

I promise that you have certain skills, talents, interests, and gifts that will not be denied. They begin to make themselves known from your earliest days, so it's just a matter of taking the time to look for and recognize them. We are all uniquely made with our own pre-packaged gifts waiting to be unwrapped. If you've ever shopped for a computer, you know that most companies offer basic models with various bundles of special features depending on your needs and interests. Some are geared to gamers like me who like to play interactive video games on their computers. Others come with sophisticated software designed for photographers, graphic artists, or financial planners.

You and I come custom-equipped in much the same way. They don't call babies *bundles of joy* for nothing. My bundle was the musical performance package. Yours may be the tech geek package, the artist package, the engineer package or the teacher package.

I encourage you to identify and develop your strengths so your weaknesses become irrelevant. Look at me. I was not a good student. My energy levels were so high that I had trouble focusing on subjects like reading, math and social studies. I was very good at daydreaming. Unfortunately they didn't grade me on that. Maybe I had attention deficit disorder that was never diagnosed. I don't know. But what I do know is that I could have studied math 24 hours a day for 365 days a year and I probably never would have done better than a C in that class. Even more important, I did not enjoy math. I never looked forward to it and I never felt good about myself while doing it—or trying to do it. A little parental encouragement would have helped, but I didn't get much of that. If I'd ask things like, "Dad do you think I could be a scientist?" the answer was likely to be, "Yeah, whatever kid."

You may have to reach down deep inside yourself and become your own source of encouragement and motivation, which is not ideal, but it certainly can be done. Build your confidence around your strong points, your talents and gifts. Just remember to make sure the young people who come into your life one day can look to you for the support they need, even if it's support you never received from your family. It's so vital for young people to have that. Try to make a difference in their lives, even if it's helping them with homework and telling them they are special in some way. Point out their strengths and encourage them to develop them.

Too many people think that the secret to happiness and success is to master their weaknesses. I think that's a recipe for a very unhappy and unsuccessful life. I'm all about focusing on strengths. There's nothing wrong with trying to improve in areas of weakness so that you can at least get by, but why devote a lot of time and effort to an area where you will never stand out or enjoy yourself?

MUSIC EXCITED ME.
I HAD A GIFT FOR IT.

You can probably guess the one subject where I did kick butt in school—music. If I could have skipped math and biology and just spent every day in the band or chorus rooms that would have been fine with me. Music excited me. I had a gift for it. So I focused on developing that strength and now if I need the skills of accountants or doctors who were wizards at math and biology, I just hire them.

I am not a failure because I'll never be a certified public accountant or be called Dr. Carter. My strengths and passions have taken me in a different direction. I can do basic math and I understand what I need to know about biology, but trying to become a "mathlete" or a biology brain would have been a waste of time for me. We have to go with our strengths if we are to be happy and fulfilled. If you love math, have a knack for numbers, study hard and become a successful accountant; who cares if you can't draw a straight line or sing on key? If you are artistic and work to become a great illustrator, graphic designer or painter, it will never matter that you stink at algebra.

READY TO ROCK

We all have our weaknesses and our strengths. I say go with what works best for you. It's about focusing on the positive so that your motivation comes from within. Devoting your time and energy to doing whatever you are inspired and passionate about, also helps you build confidence so you can overcome the challenges and setbacks that are a natural part of life.

LUCK AND TIMING—
BOTH GOOD AND BAD—PLAY A PART IN EVERY LIFE.

I would consider myself a failure only if I never tried to make the most of the gifts I've been given. That doesn't mean I had to be a pop star to find happiness. Honestly, I probably could have been very content teaching high school choir and performing weekends in clubs or for parties.

Luck and timing—both good and bad—play a part in every life. In fact, I consider myself lucky according to the theory that "Luck is where preparation meets opportunity." With my mother's help, I began building on my musical strengths from an early age with vocal coaches and dance coaches. I also performed in musical theater roles, television shows, commercials and talent competitions. So, I was about as prepared as a kid could be when luck brought the first big opportunities my way.

You may discover, as I did, that the harder you work to build your strengths, the more great opportunities will come your way, one right after the other—or even at the same time. When the Disney Channel held auditions for its "All New Mickey Mouse Club" television show produced in Orlando, I tried out. The competition for these roles was always fierce. A few names you might recognize among the other talented kids who auditioned for the show during its run from 1989 to 1995 are: Britney Spears, Jessica Simpson, Ryan Gosling, Christina Aguilera, Keri Russell and future 'N Sync stars Justin Timberlake and J.C. Chasez.

I was not only invited back for the final round of auditions for the Disney series, but another life-changing opportunity arose then, too. I learned that auditions were being held for a boy band like New Edition. An Orlando-based businessman, who just happens to be the cousin of one of my mom's favorite singers, Art Garfunkel, was behind the venture. When I heard about that connection I wondered if all those hours of singing "Bridge Over Trouble Waters" were about to pay off.

This successful entrepreneur, Lou Pearlman, had hired talent scouts to put ads in area newspapers and various entertainment-industry trade journals. Although the ads stated that his organization was looking for guys between the ages of 16 and 19, we figured it was worth a shot. They'd been conducting auditions for a couple of weeks at Pearlman's mansion, but they decided to move the screening process to a bigger venue. Pearlman, who was also in the air charter business, owned an aircraft-parts warehouse, which is where the later auditions were ultimately held. I was the first to audition in the new location, which had just the sort of acoustics you'd expect of a warehouse—not good at all.

Still, my audition went well enough that Pearlman had a long talk with my mom. He spoke about what they were looking for and the extent of the work involved. He explained that there would be long hours of rehearsing and touring and that it would be pretty demanding. During that conversation, Mom mentioned that I'd been invited back for the final auditions of "The All New Mickey Mouse Club." I don't know if she also mentioned that Disney had actually made a concrete offer in the amount of $50,000 for me to join the cast.

When we left, Mom told Lou that she and I would have to talk it all over. Since we didn't commit right away, Lou's team picked another guy as their top choice for the group. It was a good thing I didn't know about that, because when Mom and I talked that evening about which opportunity I wanted more, I told her I preferred to give the band a try.

Lucky for me, the other guy Lou's team had chosen backed out. Pearlman called a few days later and asked Mom if we were interested in joining his project. We said yes without realizing how close we'd come to missing the boat.

WORKING FOR YOURSELF

When I was selected to join the Backstreet Boys, I felt like I'd won the lottery. This was an opportunity perfectly matched for my strengths. But keep in mind that I put myself in a good position to jump on that opportunity by developing my skills; finding good mentors, teachers and role models;

listening to them; and working my butt off in practices and rehearsals, all while being on the lookout for ways to showcase my talents.

It's just like I said before: I was lucky, no doubt about it. But I was also ready to rock when luck arrived.

You need to prepare yourself, too. I'd been working since the age of eight to become what some people thought was an *overnight* success. You can't wait for the world to discover your talents. It's up to you to make people see and respond to those talents. You are responsible for your own success, happiness and fulfillment. Once you've identified your strengths and are committed to developing them, you then must find ways to motivate yourself to reach as high as you can. Again, it's all up to you. The quality of the decisions you make will determine the quality of your life.

BUT I WAS ALSO READY TO ROCK WHEN LUCK ARRIVED.

Why is identifying your talents, developing them and building your life around them so important? Because once we do those things for ourselves, we are no longer dependent on anyone else for our happiness and fulfillment. That doesn't mean you won't need other people in your life. Most of us need supportive and loving relationships. It's part of human nature. But it does mean that when people disappoint you, relationships fall apart, or hard times hit, you and I will still have our strengths to help get us through.

Again, I am the poster child for this truth. The gift of music has given me the strength to survive and thrive despite some terrible mistakes and huge challenges. I'm not being a drama king when I say it's saved my life. I began performing with Backstreet before I hit my teens. I had some talent, but I was also very young and immature to be stepping out of a Tampa junior high school and into the life of an international pop star. I didn't have the life skills to deal with the craziness that came with sudden fame, especially as I got older and fell into the same hard-partying lifestyle that my parents were into. But ultimately, focusing on my talents and being surrounded by others who took those same talents seriously helped me find my way back.

A GOOD GANG

Yes, I struggled at times and had some pretty awful episodes, but I managed to keep performing, thanks in large part to the positive and supportive members of my new musical family. One of the great rewards of building your life around your strengths and doing what you love is the friendships formed with those who share your passion. When I joined Backstreet Boys, I found myself in a new position in a new family. I was the eldest among the Carter kids but the youngest of the Backstreet Boys.

Admittedly, I was the problem child at times because of my immaturity, but I was very fortunate to join a band of brothers who stuck by me, encouraged me and cared about me. In many ways, they provided the sort of strong role models I'd never had. I've often wondered what my life would have been like if I hadn't developed my singing to the level required to make it with the Backstreet Boys. It's a little scary to think about that. Many of the kids I knew when we lived on 131st Street have had serious drug problems. Some went to prison. A few are no longer living.

Your environment can shape you. If you don't decide what you want to do with your life and go after it, you'll end up just taking what life gives you. I saw guys who didn't have much family guidance join street gangs that preyed on their weaknesses, including their lack of direction and support at home. Gang leaders are skilled at recruiting lost souls by promising to provide the *family* these kids lack. I could have ended up in a gang if my life had gone another way—if I hadn't built upon my strengths.

My mom did push me to get voice and dance lessons, and though I often feel as if she was motivated to do that because she saw the potential for more income in it, I did become a successful performer, I did find and pursue my passion, and as a result, I did end up in an entirely different sort of gang. This one was made up of guys whose drive to build upon their strengths was just as strong, or even stronger than mine.

One of the most important things I've learned in my struggle to put my life on the right track and stay there is that you have to surround yourself with people who make you want to be better—especially people who are strong where you are weak.

I didn't understand that for the longest time. Too often, I chose to hang out with people who shared my weaknesses. They didn't make me better. They weren't concerned about making themselves better either. They were out for the quick high, the cheap thrill, and the next party.

...YOU HAVE TO SURROUND YOURSELF WITH PEOPLE WHO MAKE YOU WANT TO BE BETTER.

Nobody made me run around with these negative influences. I chose to hang with them at times when I didn't want to hear what more positive and helpful people, including the guys in my band, were telling me. There are rules of attraction in science and in life too. It's a fact that when you have a negative attitude, you attract negative people, just as it is a fact that when you have a positive attitude, you attract positive people.

I've run with both crowds and there is no doubt which one is best for my career, health and spirit. It's interesting that whenever I focus on building my strengths, positive and encouraging people come into my life. When I fall to my weaknesses, the opposite is true.

So I encourage you to give serious thought to the sort of people you want to attract in your life. And remember, the people who are best for you may not always tell you what you *want* to hear, but you can count on them to tell you what you *need* to hear. I've always known that members of my surrogate family—the guys in Backstreet Boys—were there for me.

They aren't perfect saints each and every day either, but in our first years together I remember thinking, "Wow, this is what it's like to have a normal family and a normal situation." I really came to value their friendship. They wanted me to succeed and for the most part, they really were great role models.

Sometimes, though, I tuned them out because I didn't believe in myself as much as they believed in me. When BSB first formed, I grew tight with Howie Dorough right away. Even though he is seven years older than me, I hung out with him and his family a lot because Howie grew up in the Orlando area. His father, who was of Irish descent, was an Orlando police sergeant who trained police dogs and worked as a security guard to make extra money. His mother, who is of Puerto Rican descent, worked in a school cafeteria. Howie had three older sisters and an older brother, not to mention a bunch of cousins. I dated one of his nieces for a while and really got to know the whole family well.

My friendship with Howie had a positive impact on me early on. Like my own family, the Doroughs didn't have a whole lot of money, but the dynamics in their family were completely different. They were very loving toward each other. They really seemed to appreciate and care for one another. Hanging out with them, I could see where Howie got his personality. We called him Sweet D because he has this benevolence about him—a genuine, kindhearted nature.

Howie always tried to guide me and so did Brian Littrell, who, despite being five years older than me, has always been very much the old soul of our group. As a kid Brian had a lot of health problems, including a hole in his heart and a life-threatening bacterial infection. He's mature and calm, which I think is due in part to dealing with such serious health problems and also due in part to his deep religious faith. I roomed with Brian often when the group traveled in the early years. He and Howie were both like older brothers or even parents to me in those days.

Brian reminded me while we were recording in London in 2012 that my parents made him my legal guardian on one of our first European tours when I was still a minor. They trusted Brian enough to put him in charge of my welfare in case something happened on the trip. I don't think they ever told me about that, which is probably a good thing since as much as I respect Brian and felt that he was a positive role model, I never thought of him as a "father figure."

What has consistently impressed me about Brian, though, is how his entire life is built upon his Christian faith. Everything he does is guided by his spiritual beliefs. I believe in God too, but I haven't become a Christian like him. I'd never known anyone with such a strong spiritual foundation. We've had many discussions about religion and faith and I've learned a lot from him. We all have our own beliefs and interpretation of God; who is to say whether one is right or better than the others? I love science, for instance, and believe that there are scientific explanations for everything. I say count me in with Katy Perry and Megan Fox, who, like me, admit to being intrigued by the ideas raised in the History Channel show *Ancient Aliens*. I joke that the show's stories about contact between humans and ancient extraterrestrial astronauts reportedly found in historical texts, archeology and legend helps explain my own theories of religion.

Many people are afraid to talk about their faith and spirituality if they don't belong to a particular church. And some who are affiliated with a particular church are not always open to others who don't belong to that same faith. All I can say is that Brian and Kevin Richardson taught me a lot about the value of having faith to guide you and keep you on track. I've often wished that I had their strength in that regard, but I just didn't have the spiritual background they received while growing up in church-going families.

Kevin is nine years older than me, and during the first few years in the band I found him a little intimidating. I often thought of him as this big eagle looking down on me. He's very disciplined and tough-minded. Kevin was captain of his high school football team and has sort of a drill-sergeant mentality, which is good in some ways, but I didn't always respond very well to his methods. He's mellowed a lot over the years, of course, and I've also changed and grown.

I used to feel scrutinized by him, but eventually I came to realize that Kevin had my best interests at heart. As I'll talk about later in this book, he's done some things that have really helped me turn my life around. I also appreciate the fact that Kevin is always working to expand his knowledge through reading and exposing himself to new subjects and ideas. I've tried to do the same and we've had many good discussions, especially about health and nutrition.

The other member of our group, A.J. McLean, is just two years older than me. A.J. is from a background more like mine than the other guys. His parents divorced when he was four years old. His single mother raised him. He is a very creative and independent guy with a unique perspective on things.

A.J. has had issues with drugs and alcohol, like me. Kevin stepped up in a big way to help him too, leading an intervention to get A.J. into rehab and Alcoholics Anonymous. Watching A.J. go through that experience and come out of it helped me to understand the benefits of getting professional help. His example also taught me that people can make mistakes and correct their lives, but it takes a lot of work to get back on track.

The five of us may come from varied backgrounds, but we all share a love of music and a dedication to being the best we can be for ourselves and for each other. My point in telling you about my fellow band members and our relationships is that when you identify your strengths and then work to develop those talents and gifts, you attract people with similar goals and aspirations. And that's a very good thing.

THEY WILL INVEST IN YOU WHEN THEY SEE YOU INVESTING IN YOURSELF.

It has occurred to me that most of the positive and supportive people I know are those I've met through music. It's a very rare thing in this life to meet even just one or two people who truly want you to succeed. You'll find it's even rarer to find some willing to step up, tell you that you are headed in the wrong direction, and help steer you back. I've been blessed with more of those caring and trustworthy friends than I probably deserve.

The secret to attracting positive and supportive people into your life is simple: They will invest in you when they see you investing in yourself. When you work to build your strengths, you will be amazed at how many people start pulling for you, too. I know because, as I will relate in the coming chapters, I've experienced it time and again myself.

PERSONAL NOTES

CHAPTER FOUR

DRIVING BLIND

O N M Y 21ˢᵀ birthday, Kevin Richardson gave me a gift that I didn't appreciate until more than three years later. When my oldest Backstreet brother handed me the present, I scanned the title and realized it was one of the self-help books I'd seen him reading and talking a lot about. I decided immediately that the contents didn't apply to me.

I took the gift home and stuck it on a shelf with a bunch of others I hadn't yet read. I wasn't much into reading or self-help back then. I was cruising along at high speed, enjoying the lifestyle that came with being a Backstreet Boy and selling millions of records. Those first eight years were amazing.

THOSE FIRST EIGHT YEARS WERE AMAZING.

But the other members of the group were older and seemed to be settling down. In fact, a couple of the guys were talking about getting married and starting families. Not me. I'd just hit legal drinking age and figured it was my time to party. I also was enjoying being single for the first time in three years. I'd been dating another singer from the Tampa area, Amanda Williford, whose performing name was Willa Ford, but we broke up in late 2000. I figured since I'd reached the age when most guys were in college, drinking, partying and chasing women, that having that kind of fun should be my mission too.

I didn't want to stop and think about where I was headed. I just wanted to enjoy the moment and live life as much as possible.

When Kevin gave me that birthday gift in January 2001, we were on our Black & Blue Tour, promoting our fourth album, which like our third had sold more than a million copies in its first week—a record for back-to-back albums. We'd just done a huge concert in Atlanta and were headed to Philadelphia for the next tour date. But first we made a little birthday stop in my hometown.

We celebrated my big day by singing the national anthem at Raymond James Stadium for the pre-game ceremony at Super Bowl XXXV. It was extra special because my favorite quarterback Trent Dilfer, a good friend who used to play for Tampa Bay, was playing for the Baltimore Ravens (and they beat the New York Giants in the game!).

More than 71,000 fans packed the stands and another 84 million watched on television. That wasn't a bad way to kick off what proved to be a great year for our group. We spent 11 months of 2001 touring the United States, Canada, South America and Japan. The Black & Blue Tour grossed $100 million worldwide, so things were going well financially, too.

We also felt good about our future because we'd ended our contract with Lou Pearlman, who'd been taking a double helping of our earnings. Our contract paid him once as our manager and again as the "sixth member" of our group. We'd been grateful for all "Big Poppa" had done early on to help the band get started and to build our fan base. Over time, though, we all came to see that Pearlman was not the benevolent father figure he'd appeared to be when we first signed our management agreement with him.

Big Poppa was yet another father figure in my life who proved untrustworthy. At first, some fans and music industry people who didn't know the whole story criticized us and called us ungrateful for severing ties with him. Soon though, his shady dealings became matters of public record because of a federal investigation that sent him to prison.

The way I see it, we had a business relationship with Lou Pearlman and we ended it. We had viewed him as a mentor and a friend, but nothing more. He never made any sexual advances toward me or toward the other band members, as far as I know, despite rumors to the contrary. As young artists trying to launch our careers, we entered into a deal with him gladly, and we ended it even more gladly. I now look at our dealings with him as a lesson learned. He had offered us the opportunity of a lifetime—we had no other access to major labels, recording studios or concert promoters. We trusted Pearlman until we realized that was a mistake.

I NOW LOOK AT OUR DEALINGS WITH HIM AS A LESSON LEARNED.

As the saying goes, "Fool me once, shame on you. Fool me twice, shame on me." We all make mistakes and we all experience failure. This is especially true when we are young and less experienced in the ways of the world. The music business is complex. It's also true that no one could have foreseen just how successful the Backstreet Boys would become and how much income we would generate.

LIVE AND LEARN

Our dealings and disappointments with Lou Pearlman taught us to be much more careful about the people we trusted and the contracts we signed. I have no interest in living with regret over that or any of my other mistakes, failures, or setbacks. You shouldn't either. My goal is to remain focused on the future and the greater possibilities for my life.

Similarly, I encourage you to stay positive even when you make mistakes and experience failures. You have to be realistic and acknowledge when you've messed up, or fallen short of your goals and expectations. You also have to be aware that there are predatory people who will try to take advantage of you. You can't ignore the bad, but you can choose to live in the good.

Remember that you have the power to choose a positive attitude even when negative things happen to you. When you do that, you'll discover that good things can come even from the worst experiences. I tended to dwell on the dark side before I took responsibility for my own happiness and success and believe me, life is much better in the light of optimism.

You can't ignore mistakes or disappointments, as that's just not very realistic. But you can't allow them to throw you off permanently either. So ask yourself, "Who would you rather be?" The person who never gets over mistakes, or the person who acknowledges them, learns from them, corrects what needs to be corrected, and uses the experience to build an even better life?

WE ONLY HAVE SO MUCH TIME ON THIS EARTH, AND WE ALL FALL SHORT NOW AND THEN.

Being bitter and negative only compounds the damage, so why do that to yourself? Maybe you messed up. Maybe someone took advantage of you, or you didn't do all you should have done to accomplish a goal. What I try to do in those circumstances is learn from it, get over it, and get on with it. We only have so much time on this earth, and we all fall short now and then. Sometimes we even land flat on our faces. But we have a choice in what we do next. We can stay down there in the dirt or we can just keep getting back up until the final count. I like option number two. How about you?

THE BLOOPER REEL

So many of us laugh at bloopers on television shows and movies because messing up is a universal experience. We all trip over our own feet at times. We all turn right when we should have turned left. Screwing up in some way, shape, or form is a daily occurrence. We never grow out of that awkward stage. Goofing up is part of life. Yes, you and I will create our own WTF moments until we draw our last breaths.

Life coaches and therapists encourage us to welcome our mistakes and failures because they provide learning opportunities. That's not always easy, but it's a good goal and makes a lot of sense. Most successful people will tell you that their greatest achievements were built upon trial and error. Look at scientists—they make a living learning from failed experiments. Mathematicians also work their way through wrong solutions to find the right ones. The best quarterbacks in the NFL rarely complete more than 70 percent of their passes.

Still, I have a tough time when I make mistakes because they often have a negative impact or cause considerable pain for myself or for someone else. Screwing up is embarrassing. You may blame yourself or you may fear others will blame you. Sometimes you might feel like you will never recover from a failure or mistake. Often, people who've messed up only make things worse with exaggerated statements like, "My life is over." Or, "I'm dead."

Drama doesn't help. Neither does equating our mistakes and failures with dying. In fact, the only people who can't make mistakes are those who are six feet under. Making mistakes and having problems is part of living, so acknowledge the truth in that and deal with it. Accept that you will make mistakes and look at them as opportunities to learn and become better.

WHENEVER I MESS UP MY FIRST INSTINCT IS TO KICK MYSELF.

Therapists have told me that one of the secrets to dealing with all mistakes and failures is to not personalize them. Honestly, I didn't know that you could choose to not take a mistake personally. Whenever I mess up my first instinct is to kick myself. Most the time I just want to beat my head against a wall even if it is something as common as forgetting the lyrics to a song.

THE BLAME GAME

So how exactly do you de-personalize your own dumb moves and miserable flops? The answer is simple: by focusing on what happened, rather than who is to blame. Think of it as letting yourself out of jail. If you want to spend a couple of minutes behind bars (I mean figuratively, not in

San Quentin or anything), that's fine, but then post bond and bust out. Examine where you went wrong, commit to making it right or to making a better choice next time, and then move forward.

You don't need to keep score either. Just drive on. Let the past fade out of sight in the rear view mirror, and focus on the road ahead. You can't change what happened, but you can control how you respond. When thinking about my biggest blunders and bust-ups I prefer to hold onto this thought: I can use my failures and mistakes as opportunities to get better and be better.

I find it crazy that we are often willing to forgive our friends and loved ones for screwing up yet we refuse to forgive ourselves. I'll write more about the awesome power of forgiveness later. Just remember for now that this simple act has many great uses, and one of the most important is the self-application. If you aren't at least as good a friend to yourself as you are to others then you need to work on loving that person in the mirror.

YET, I KEPT MESSING UP AND LETTING MY MISTAKES DRAG ME DOWN FARTHER AND FARTHER.

Simple to state, tough to do, I know.

For the longest time I beat myself up over every little thing. I was like a one man fight club. There are two wrong ways to handle mistakes. One is to pay no attention to them at all and just keep making them. The other is to get all angry and depressed but not learn from them or make corrections. I did all of the above in my early years with Backstreet Boys.

There I was, living a dream come true. Millions of talented people would have given anything to be in our group. Yet, I kept messing up and letting my mistakes drag me down farther and farther. Many of my screw-ups were understandable or even unavoidable. I was so young when we began touring the world. I entered my teen years—those years when we are expected to make mistakes—as a celebrity pop star who made the tabloids, fan magazines and Internet news every time I flirted with the wrong girl, forgot to leave a tip, or was caught in the wrong club. Tabloid writers and celebrity-stalking reporters made up some of the stuff they wrote about me, but I also made mistakes that the public never learned about.

BAD MOVES

Kevin and the other BSB members saw me drinking and getting in trouble and all they could do was shake their heads. Howie nailed it when he told a reporter a few years ago, "Sometimes the last people you want to take advice from are the people closest to you. Nick was on a journey to find himself. When he was scolded, rather than motivating him, he curled up and crawled into a darker hole."

...I BEGAN MY HEADLONG DIVE INTO THAT DEEP DARK HOLE...

They told me that I had the potential to be a better person and to make more of my talents. They knew I had a good heart and soul, but I wasn't using my head. The guys warned me many times that my partying was out of control and that I was headed for serious trouble. They worried that I could destroy my career and seriously damage theirs, too.

Yet, when the other members of Backstreet tried to help me, I fought them tooth and nail. Looking back, I realize I should have been much more accountable to them, not just from a business standpoint but because they cared about me as a person. My party-hearty lifestyle stayed under wraps for a long time because I did my drinking and drugs out of public view most of the time. Then, when I finally reached legal drinking age, I began my headlong dive into that deep dark hole Howie referred to.

My downward spiral became news when I was arrested in January of 2002 at the Pop City bar in Tampa. I'd gone there with a group of local friends. We hit it hard and then things got out of control near closing time. We were just a bunch of normal guys doing the things guys do to get in trouble. Of course, I should have been more aware of my responsibility as a member of Backstreet. I should not have been acting irresponsibly or doing unhealthy things, but I was trying to fit in with a group of friends who were not really the best influences. I was a product of my environment at that time. After touring with the group and living in that warped reality of being a celebrity and traveling constantly, I wanted to return to a more "normal" lifestyle, but in truth, the binge drinking, drug use and partying all the time wasn't really a normal existence either.

THE HEADLINE IN THE NEW YORK POST LATER READ, "BACKSTREET BOOZER BUSTED FOR BRAWL."

My memories of that night are very hazy. As I recall, we were at the bar and getting ready to leave because it was closing time. We were drunk. I yelled something at a bartender that was rude and they kicked me out of the club. People messed with me on the way out, yelling things, and it caused a scene. Once I got outside I headed to the valet parking area. I really was trying to avoid trouble and just get my car and leave. But then this guy came up and started hassling me. He was probably just trying to get me to clear out, but I didn't care. He was wearing a jacket and I couldn't tell if he had a uniform on or not, but I later saw that he had a badge. He was telling me to get in this car and I was very, very confrontational with him. I kept asking who he was and why I should listen to him.

My friends were yelling, "Do what he says, he's a cop!"

I was so drunk. I didn't realize he was an officer until it was too late and he slammed me up against the vehicle telling me that I was under arrest. People from the bar were laughing at me and it was this big scene. It was so embarrassing.

After the cop said I was under arrest, I tried to act tough to impress my friends. At first, I thought being arrested was sort of cool, but once you get thrown into the backseat of a police car and they lock the door, you realize what's really happening and your view quickly changes. This was just another example of my not caring enough about my responsibilities and not learning from my mistakes.

I realized that I'd lost control of myself and I remember crying on the way to the station. I was so embarrassed. I said, "I'm sorry, I'm sorry, please don't do this."

The headline in the New York Post later read, "Backstreet Boozer Busted For Brawl." The tabloids portrayed me as doing everything from grabbing a security guy by the neck to exposing myself—none of which was true.

The police charged me with a misdemeanor of "resisting arrest without violence" apparently because "drunk and belligerent" wasn't a category. My memory of that night is fuzzy, for good reason. The Tampa police said they asked me to quiet down more than ten times and I refused each time. They claimed that they gave me a three-count to get out of the bar and I still didn't leave. So they handcuffed me and put me in a squad car.

I was ashamed, of course. I defended myself on MTV's *Total Request Live* (TRL) and on other occasions, saying that I just didn't move quickly enough when an officer told me to clear out of the bar. I apologized to the Tampa Police Department, the members of BSB and our fans. Basically, I was just trying to uphold my reputation and do whatever damage control I could. TRL host Carson Daly said being arrested would probably help my reputation. I guess Carson thought I needed to rough up the Backstreet Boys' image and be more of a bad ass. I'm pretty sure Carson had me on to help his ratings, but on some level, I thought maybe he was right and something positive could potentially come of this mistake. Unfortunately, I didn't learn from it. I just kept compounding my problems by continuing the same unacceptable behavior and messing up. No internal alarms went off for me, despite what the other guys in Backstreet said. I rolled on, repeating the same self-destructive pattern for quite a while longer.

The previous summer A.J. McLean had entered rehab. But A.J. did something that I refused to do. He acknowledged his mistakes and began correcting them. Now, he's human and he's slipped up a few times, returning to rehab again in 2002 and more recently in 2011. My heart goes out to him. I have nothing but admiration and empathy for his efforts to face his demons. A.J. and I have discussed our shared battles many times. He has helped me more than he will ever know. I'm incredibly grateful to him.

ARRESTED DEVELOPMENT

After the incident in Tampa, I could tell that my BSB family felt I'd let them down and that I was hurting our relationship. As the "baby" in BSB, I never wanted to disappoint or harm our group in any way. But my responsibility to the others was something I couldn't seem to handle for the longest time. Even though I loved my "job" and my bandmates, I kept messing up. I was self-sabotaging, in part because I didn't feel like I deserved the fans' respect and affection. They loved me, but I didn't much love myself at that point.

Some of it was just the typical rebelliousness most young guys with a lot of energy and a false sense of immortality experience. This was around the time I asserted my independence as a member of BSB by opting to stay with The Firm management group after the other members left that agency. I also decided to make a solo album, which turned out to be *Now Or Never*. The other guys weren't happy with those decisions, but I was angry at the world. I had it in my head that music was the way to vent that anger.

THEY LOVED ME, BUT I DIDN'T MUCH LOVE MYSELF AT THAT POINT.

I really wasn't concerned about the repercussions of my actions or the feelings they'd stir in others. I was very selfish. I actually felt resentful toward Backstreet because I'd spent so much time and energy on my career, I believed I was missing out on other things. I didn't appreciate all that being in the group had done for me. I was more focused on what I thought I'd lost.

I wanted to write songs about my feelings and use the solo tour as an outlet for them. I went on the road and did just that, screaming at the top of my lungs as I sang track after track from my album. I don't know how the audience felt, but it was very therapeutic for me. The first single released was "Help Me" and though I didn't write it, the chorus reflected my state of mind:

Help me

Figure out the difference

Between right and wrong

Weak and strong

Day and night

Where I belong and

Help me

Make the right decisions

Know which way to turn

Lessons to learn

And just what my purpose is here

The songs on my *Now Or Never* solo album truly helped me to get over those feelings of resentment and anger. It was like writing a diary and then reading it to thousands of people. I wanted *everyone* to know what I was going through. I wanted them to hear my pain. It was the only way I knew how to fully express myself. It was sad, really. I was this overweight, unhealthy solo artist who was sweating profusely and wearing clothes on stage that I could barely fit into. It was heart-wrenching. I almost ruined my relationship with BSB over it. I was so mentally unhealthy at the time I wouldn't let family members come around me.

I WANTED THEM TO HEAR
MY PAIN.

Then again, if I hadn't done the solo album and expressed those feelings, I might never have been able to distinguish what was good in my life from what was bad. I discovered that a lot of fans related to my pain and anger because they had gone through similar challenges. They could feel my angst and so many of the lyrics hit home for them. The album did well, but I wish I had been more prepared for that solo venture, more responsible and healthy. I think I could have appreciated the experience more and made the most of the opportunity it represented.

I did learn from many of the mistakes I made during that time though. For example, I discovered that I wasn't prepared to handle the workload that comes with a solo career. I didn't have a plan and I wasn't comfortable in a position that required me to direct people and be the leader. I thought I could just cut some songs and let my manager do all the work, but that's not the way it is.

In some respects, I'm glad that my solo career didn't take off with that album. Who knows what might have happened? I might not have made the decision to change my lifestyle and behavior. Things worked out with Backstreet. I'm much happier and healthier now than I have been in many years and am thrilled to be celebrating 20 years of hard work and success with the group.

I was stepping out in a lot of ways during that solo period. It occurred right around the time my parents finally divorced. I had a lot of mixed feelings about that. My father and I had developed more of a friendship than we had previously, but I was uncomfortable when he asked me for money and advice. Aaron's efforts to assert his financial and career independence also forced me to choose sides. Naturally, I sided with my brother because I'd been through the same issues with our parents as he'd gone through.

When I became a celebrity at such a young age no one handed me an instruction manual or warnings about how to behave under the media spotlight. I felt like I was under a magnifying glass and that people were judging me all the time. The pressure got to me. The only place I was comfortable was on stage or in the studio. The rest of the time I wanted to run away and hide. I just wished I could be "normal." I remember the conflict of having huge responsibility, success and power, but not feeling worthy of it. It seemed that I craved normalcy so much because I felt I didn't deserve what I had been given. That attitude caused me to be irresponsible with my money and my relationships and my life. I rebelled against everyone's expectations of me. The immaturity, insecurities and bad habits I had learned in childhood quickly led to turmoil and trouble.

THE DOWNWARD SPIRAL

When you fail to learn from your mistakes, you don't only repeat them, you inevitably crash and burn. I was headed for such a crash and burn after my 21st birthday. Nobody was trying to shoot me down. I was the one "piloting my own plane" so to speak, and heading for certain disaster.

Marijuana was my starter drug, after alcohol, and then I moved into my Ecstasy phase, and prescription painkillers in my early twenties. I did a lot of Ecstasy over one particular three or four month period and I probably regret taking that illegal and dangerous drug more than anything I've done. I'm afraid the amount I did caused chemical changes in my brain that are responsible for bouts of depression that I now struggle to control.

THE PRESSURE
GOT TO ME.

Like I said earlier, I thought I was invincible, just as many young people do. I was wrong. None of us are immune to the side effects of these drugs. Even if you disregard every other piece of advice I give you in this book, please take to heart my warnings about Ecstasy. This is a drug that can destroy your brain and ruin your life. I'm lucky that it hasn't had a worse impact on me. But who knows what the effects will be down the road? It's very scary to think about that because my brain already seems to operate differently than it did before.

Because of the problems I had after using this illegal drug, known scientifically as MDMA, I've done some research into it and found that it increases the activity of serotonin in the brain, which regulates mood, sleep, pain, emotion, and appetite. The increased serotonin causes the high that comes with taking Ecstasy. The problem is that the high lasts about two or three hours while the negative after-effects can last much longer. The negative effects include anxiety, paranoia, vertigo, memory problems and depression. People who use Ecstasy a lot often talk about having dark moods or overwhelming sadness for days or weeks afterward. And that's not the worst problem with Ecstasy. There have been studies suggesting that the more you use it, the more you can damage your brain, maybe even permanently. It also has the potential to affect your body temperature so dramatically that it could lead to heart failure and even death. Some studies have also found that Ecstasy can interact with other drugs—especially uppers or stimulants—to kill you. It can potentially raise your body temperature high enough to trigger hypothermia.

As with many illegal street drugs, you never know what you are getting when you buy what you think is Ecstasy. It's pretty common for dealers to mix MDMA with amphetamines, caffeine or ephedrine to stretch their supply and make more money. Then there are those people mixing Ecstasy with alcohol, pot and other drugs simultaneously, which is crazy. Please hear what I'm saying, take my warnings seriously, and stay away from drugs, especially those that can permanently alter your brain functions and your behavior.

HIGH LIVING

One of the mistakes I made during this period of time was not removing myself from the environment or the sort of people that fed my worst impulses as far as drinking, drugs and partying are concerned. My membership in Backstreet Boys took me into a world I was not prepared for. The temptations I encountered were far greater after I became known as a pop singer. They came at me in a mad rush that never seemed to stop. Hollywood and Beverly Hills were not the places for me to be at that particular stage of my life and career. Neither were the Hamptons, Park Avenue, Greenwich Village, or any other haunts of the rich and shameless.

Paris Hilton was probably the worst person in the world for me to hook up with at that time. And of course, I did just that.

I'm not putting her down at all. She is a great lady in many ways that most people aren't even aware of. She just wasn't the right one for me to be with at that shaky point in my life. We grew up in different worlds— at times it even felt like different planets. I didn't choose my parents or my family and she didn't choose hers. It's just that all of her life, Paris has been able to have anything she's wanted. That was not my reality. So, while we shared certain interests in music, movies, travel and other things, our perceptions and expectations were very different. I think in some ways, we became each other's crutches. We leaned on each other because we were not sure of ourselves. We were young and the relationship was something new and fun, but the truth of the matter is, when you go chasing waterfalls sometimes you end up in an empty river. I'm just a normal dude, no matter what I do for a living. I enjoy simple guy things like video games and music. From my perspective, Paris's lifestyle was over the top—just too extreme for me.

There's no doubt that Paris and I had a strong mutual attraction physically. We dated for seven months or so in 2003, so there was obviously a connection. But early in our relationship she told a friend of mine that she posted my pictures on her walls when she was a teenager. I believe she saw me as that pop star instead of the regular guy I really am underneath it all. I wasn't surprised, but it still made me a little uncomfortable. Paris didn't date blue-collar dudes. She's always dated celebrities and other rich and famous people.

WE LEANED ON EACH OTHER BECAUSE WE WERE NOT SURE OF OURSELVES.

I think she saw being a celebrity as a means to an end. Many other people feel the same way and I say "God bless 'em," but I wasn't as interested in being famous as I was in making music and entertaining people, building on my strengths and using my gifts. Fame is just something that came with success as an entertainer. I want to do things that uplift people and make a difference in their lives.

Still, for better or worse, Paris saw me as a celebrity and therefore as her "type." I'll admit that I was curious about her and her lavish lifestyle. Who wouldn't be? But I quickly realized that I didn't belong in her jet-set crowd.

I'll never forget going with her to Puffy's (Sean 'P. Diddy' Combs) Fourth of July White Party in the Hamptons in 2004. We flew in on this helicopter. I had never arrived at a party that way before. I hate helicopters. When I first performed with BSB in Germany, we were supposed to ride in one with some kids for a charity event. We missed the take-off time and the helicopter went down, killing almost everybody onboard. For a long time, I was so petrified at the thought of that happening again. But I put that thought out of my mind on the evening of the party and we safely landed on the property of a 12,500 square foot mansion owned by Sony. The mansion was situated on six acres in Bridgehampton and was called the PlayStation 2 Estate. Paris was supposedly co-hosting along with Puffy and Jay-Z. We weren't getting along that day. I felt like a fish out of water. It was strange for me because I remember sitting down on a couch looking around not knowing anybody while she was socializing with everybody. In many ways I didn't want to be there. I felt uncomfortable and out of place—like a lost puppy, not knowing what to do, or who to talk to. Maybe that's because I was abandoned for hours on end while she did her thing.

FAME IS JUST SOMETHING THAT CAME WITH SUCCESS AS AN ENTERTAINER.

I might have had a better experience if I hadn't gone with her. I felt that night as if I was being looked at as her boy toy. I'm sure that if I went back to that place now by myself, with my new healthier lifestyle and mentality, I would probably fit in better. I was there with someone I wasn't convinced really cared about me. I often felt like she was playing me, but that no one would tell me so. I had tried getting out of the relationship several times because I couldn't shake the feeling that stuff was going on behind my back.

There were people in those ultra-rich, society circles who seemed fake and soulless to me. After being exposed to that lifestyle for a while, I decided it wasn't healthy for me to stay there or to continue my relationship with Paris.

Living like that just wasn't for me. I admit, that hanging around with people who are willing to take you along for that kind of pampered ride can be very seductive at first, but personally, I didn't want to get too caught up in it for too long.

Paris and I went our separate ways mostly because of our different views on life. This was one instance when I recognized that staying in an unhealthy relationship and environment was a mistake, so I got out. But during this time, I made many other mistakes, and often compounded them.

OPPORTUNITIES LOST

One of my long-time goals has been to move into film and television acting, so when I was cast in the 2004 television movie *The Hollow*, I was happy to be taking a first big step in that direction. But one of the serious mistakes I alluded to above is that I squandered this opportunity by failing to maintain focus. It was the ideal chance to really develop my acting abilities. Instead, I partied way too hard.

One night, another actor in the movie went to Santa Monica Beach with me and we went overboard in a really big way. We sat next to the pier and drank until we nearly passed out. I brought my guitar and was playing, but I couldn't stop drinking. We had started at my apartment by downing about ten Flaming Dr. Peppers made with 151-proof rum (75 percent alcohol, twice the normal level) and almond-flavored liqueur dropped into a beer.

...THAT I SQUANDERED THIS OPPORTUNITY BY FAILING TO MAINTAIN FOCUS.

We were lighting them on fire and drinking one after another even before we headed to the beach. I took the bottle of rum with us to the pier and then we just drank and drank until I blacked out. When I woke up, I was back in my apartment and scared as hell because I didn't know how I got there or what had happened during the time in between. Blacking out like that was typical when I was drinking heavily.

I think I had alcohol poisoning because I got sick as soon as I woke up. I crawled into the bathroom and just stayed on the floor for three or four hours, thinking I was going to die. Then for some reason I decided I needed to eat. The only thing I could find in the kitchen was a box of Cheerios. I ate the whole box, still thinking I'd never survive this.

I had to work on *The Hollow* set that night but because I hadn't studied my lines or gotten any sleep, I went in unprepared, sick, and looking terrible. I took this opportunity for granted instead of preparing for it and making the most of it. I was still able to do my thing, but my face was so swollen, I can see how unhealthy and tired I was in the final film. Even though I somehow made it through the night, I know I acted very irresponsibly. I could have done a lot better.

Sure, I memorized my lines for the movie. I showed up and did the work, yet I still feel badly that I didn't maximize the experience. Had I committed myself to doing my best, my performance could have helped me establish the acting career I wanted. Instead, I partied on, as if my goal wasn't important to me at all. This was another low point for me in many ways. My mind was going places I didn't want it to go. I'd be driving somewhere and find my thoughts had wandered to very dark scenarios. It was as if my subconscious was searching for ways to create drama and negativity.

MY MIND WAS GOING PLACES I DIDN'T WANT IT TO GO.

One night I was doing prescription painkillers on top of drinking alcohol and I remember going back to my condo, getting in bed alone, listening to my heart pound and feeling as if my body was falling apart from the inside out. I was paranoid at times, worrying that if my heart were to stop no one would even care that I died. The thought kept striking me that my death would be chronicled as just another *celebrity* tragedy, one more tale of drug abuse and a waste of life and talent.

But despite those fears, I never seemed to learn from my mistakes.

DRIVING TO DISASTER

Never Gone, the first Backstreet Boys album since our two-year hiatus, was set for release in the summer of 2005. We were deep into rehearsals for a promotional tour that would include 79 concerts in the U.S., Canada, Europe, Asia and Australia. I needed to be on top of my game. But as you

A FEW PICS I'D LIKE TO SHARE

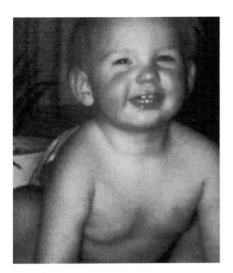

Cheese!

Wasn't I a cutie?

My passion for music started at a young age.

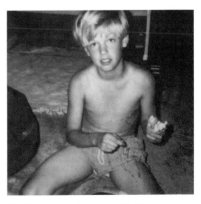

Goofing around in Casa de Carter.

I've always been a dog person.

Learning my ABCs!

I've always loved shooting hoops.

My parents say I'm a natural born ham.

Me, age 12, rocking some sweet 90's fashion.

Me and my sister BJ on vacation.

Little me, giving a kitten a lift.

Dyeing eggs with Grandpa Neal!

Me and Lauren enjoying a tasty treat.

Me and the boys, A.J. McLean, Brian Littrell, Howie
Dorough and Kevin Richardson, in the early days of BSB.

From left: Brian, A.J., me, and Howie performing at the 2010 American Music Awards show.

Me and the boys at the 2010 American Music Awards.

Me and the guys in 2013 accepting our Hollywood Walk of Fame star.

We were all so young when BSB first started!

These guys have always had my back, through thick and thin, and that means the world to me.

I feel so at home when I'm on stage.

might have guessed by now, I wasn't. I was overweight and out of shape and badly needed to get my act together.

Instead, I took a nosedive deeper into despair.

On a rare day off from meetings and rehearsals, I went with some friends to the Newport Beach and Huntington Beach area to party all day. I liked getting out of town so I could do my own thing and not get caught. I also loved the beach there.

I TOOK A NOSEDIVE DEEPER INTO DESPAIR.

On the way down, my friends and I were listening to heavy metal music in my car. At that point it was a genre I could really relate to. I felt like it was speaking right to me. We were getting so into it, we were head-banging and acting really crazy. Now mind you, I love all music and I'm a big fan of hard rock bands such as System of a Down, Slipknot and Metallica to name a few, so I'm not saying that heavy metal music was the culprit. It was *not* the reason I behaved the way I did that day or any other day. But when you have a lot of hate and anger festering inside you, you find a way to feed it and, sadly, the lyrics to some songs are what hate and anger can sometimes sink their teeth into. Yet, for every person who uses heavy metal or rap music to fuel his or her anger, there's a person out there who is perfectly capable of listening to that same music and separating entertainment from reality. A healthy mind can do that. Unfortunately, my mind and emotions weren't healthy at the time. In fact, they were out of control when we pulled up to valet park at a waterfront restaurant near the pier on Huntington Beach. We had been doing this routinely for a couple of weeks during my breaks, meeting with friends and going to a series of bars in the area. We'd play pool and drink away the day, doing shots until we lost track of time. Some of the bar staff seemed to be afraid of us because we were so wild. We finally got kicked out of one place, so we hit another bar and that's where I started having black outs. The more I drank, the more agitated and upset I became. I felt these waves of rage and resentment toward my parents. The feelings just boiled up from inside me. I couldn't stop thinking about how I missed out on a lot of fun in my teen years because I had to work so hard to please and support my family. The thought that I had to make up for lost time kept racing obsessively through my brain.

Apparently I decided that the way to recover those years was to binge drink myself blind. I justified my behavior by telling myself these were the equivalent to my college years. Whenever I drank, I became vulnerable to those unresolved feelings about my parents' drinking and fighting and their lack of nurturing. Then, I'd repeat their behavior by drinking and fighting, too.

We can easily fall into the lifestyle patterns that are most familiar to us, as I've said before. My parents drank, so I drank. They fought, so I fought. They had dysfunctional relationships, and so did I.

THE MORE I DRANK, THE MORE AGITATED AND UPSET I BECAME.

But because of my success with Backstreet and the fame and money it generated, I attracted lots of people who brought out the worst in me. I knew that I was in bad company, making bad decisions, and headed for a crash and burn, yet I did nothing to prevent that from happening. One mistake led to another and another until this day turned into one of my darkest.

At the last bar, I was so drunk and on the edge of passing out once again that I found myself on the bathroom floor. I was totally fixated on the music we'd been blasting in the car on the way down from Santa Monica. The more we drank, the more satanic the songs seemed. Normally, the battle between good and evil isn't a major topic of debate in my mind, but on this day my alcohol-and drug-induced mood rapidly brought the music's blaring negative messages back—its lyrics pounding punches to my head.

The songs were loaded with references to the devil and they were freaking me out. Obliterated out of my mind, with disturbing images and thoughts circling inside my skull like bats, I found myself wondering: What's so bad about the devil anyway? Why was Satan really thrown out of heaven? Could it all have been just a big misunderstanding?

The mind is a terrible thing to waste and wasted I was. I suddenly realized I was thinking out loud, too. A crowd that included my drunken friends and total strangers had gathered in the bathroom listening to me rant about the devil and the dark side. I felt like I was in a bottomless, black pit. People were looking at me as if snakes were crawling out of my ears.

Why is bad so bad? Why is evil, evil? Why does Satan get such a bum rap?

Now, these aren't necessarily bad questions for a theology or philosophy class to ponder, but I was just a babbling drunk sprawled next to the urinals. Then to make matters worse, I went mobile. Somehow I rose up, stumbled out of the bathroom and the bar, and made my way to the beachfront restaurant where I had valet-parked my BMW 750 that morning (though it seemed like two weeks earlier).

The valet took one look at me in full meltdown mode and, to his credit, said, "I'm not giving you the car keys."

THE MIND IS A TERRIBLE THING TO WASTE AND WASTED I WAS.

I went off on the guy, even though he was just doing his job and trying to save me from killing myself or someone else, but he was not intimidated. I calmed myself and after a brief flash of coherent thought I promised him that I'd let one of my friends drive.

One member of my posse managed to imitate a sober person long enough to win the car keys. He drove two blocks, stopped the car, handed me the keys, and we switched places.

We thought we were brilliant badasses at that point, but I only drove a few blocks before I had second thoughts and pulled to the side of the road to try and sober up.

We were still parked and listening to music when a convoy of Huntington Beach police cars with screaming sirens surrounded us. I suspected that the parking valet called the cops, and if he did, I am incredibly grateful to him. He may have saved my life or the lives of others.

At least that's how I feel now. But when those patrol cars came roaring down on us, I wasn't quite so awash in gratitude. The police officers didn't mess around. They gave me a sobriety field test, which I failed with flying colors.

It was only about 7:30 at night, but we'd had an early start. We'd set out that morning dedicated to drinking ourselves stupid. Mission accomplished.

This marked my first visit to a jail as a guest of dishonor. They had me in a holding cell by myself. I was right behind the area where the cops were working and walking by with other people they'd arrested. I was on display for everyone to see. I felt like a trapped rat. I just wanted to crawl into a hole and hide.

I FELT LIKE A
TRAPPED RAT.

They held me for about eight hours before releasing me. No one came to get me. I had to find a cab to take my sorry butt home. This was a new low, though not the lowest point I'd fall to. Looking back, I feel like maybe I was being tested in a way. I was fixated on evil and I got arrested. The devil gave me what I'd asked for. Maybe if I'd been thinking good thoughts, I would have experienced something better.

I'd like to tell you that I learned from this terrible mistake and immediately turned my life around, that I stopped drinking and doing drugs right then and there. Unfortunately, that was not the case. I'd screwed up badly, but I wasn't yet ready to learn from that awful event, change my lifestyle and move forward.

The judge who heard my case did force me to take one good step in that direction, however, by ordering me to attend Alcoholics Anonymous meetings. Getting to those meetings was a pain in the ass because I was on a crazy schedule preparing for the tour and all of the promotional events surrounding the release of the new album. But the judge didn't care. He was trying to do for me what I could not do for myself.

The court mandated that I attend thirteen meetings. I made them all. Although the Alcoholics Anonymous program has seen millions of people like me, I was not one of their great success stories—at least not right away. But they definitely succeeded in turning on some lights where there had been only darkness before.

Finally, I began to acknowledge what I'd known for some time but had ignored—that alcohol is an addictive drug and a depressant, not a happiness potion, and certainly not a cure for all the insecurities and resentments I'd harbored since childhood. To be honest, I resisted much of what they said in the first AA meetings because like a lot of young people, I thought their material didn't apply to me. I didn't think I was an alcoholic. I just liked to party. I drank and got drunk, but I felt sure that I could shut it off at any time.

HE WAS TRYING TO DO FOR ME WHAT I COULD NOT DO FOR MYSELF.

The AA folks had heard all of that before. In fact, they've heard every lame excuse and seen every form of denial there is. They ignored my ignorance and did their best to save me from myself. They had a tough job though, because I still didn't know what I did not know.

In those AA sessions, I at least learned about the science of alcohol and its impact on the body, mind and spirit. They also taught me about *windows of opportunities*, when we are given the chance to change the direction of our lives. Some people hit bottom and it still isn't low enough for them. Don't let that happen to you.

I kept pushing help away until I sunk even deeper into that black hole I keep mentioning, which was becoming an increasingly scary place.

After my DUI arrest, I blew the opportunity to pick up the pieces and move on. As a result, I made even bigger errors. I am very lucky to have survived.

I AM VERY LUCKY TO HAVE SURVIVED.

Still, after completing the AA course, I told everybody I was a changed man. I may have believed it for a while, but after a short time I went back into full party mode.

The one lesson that did resonate with me was that I shouldn't drink and drive anymore, which was good, but not good enough.

PERSONAL NOTES

CHAPTER FIVE

THE NIGHT OF THE ZOMBIES

I FINALLY HIT rock bottom one night in 2006. I was 26 years old and for nearly half my life I'd been tunneling my way deeper and deeper into denial's dark crevice. The sad irony, of course, is that while I was self-destructing through my alcohol and drug abuse, I was also living my dream and the dream of countless others as a member of the Backstreet Boys. I had it all and damned near blew the whole deal.

My life plummeted to an all-time low on what I call my *night of the zombies*. My Hollywood crowd of friends was into binge drinking in a big way, which was common not just in our social circles but also across the country. Binge drinking is generally defined as having more than five alcoholic drinks during a three-hour period, resulting in acute impairment. Nearly all the young binge drinkers that I've known drink far more booze than that in a night. Many also up the ante and increase the health risks by taking drugs like cocaine, Ecstasy, methamphetamines or smoking pot too.

We'd chug beers and pound down shot after shot until we reached the semi-comatose state where the alcohol made us sleepy and lethargic. Then we'd do a bump of cocaine for an energy boost. A couple of cans of Red Bull would have been cheaper, legal, and not nearly as hazardous to our health, I know, but binge drinkers aren't known for their common sense.

My crowd made partying an extreme sport. We repeated that binge and bump cycle night after night. After a few months we were hardly functioning. I felt as if I was nothing more than a shell wrapped around a hollow core.

More than once I thought: *I might as well be dead.* The bottom came on a night that started out like every other since I'd moved into a Santa Monica house with a friend. We hit the circuit, stopping first at a recording studio party, and then moving to some clubs before returning to the studio party to close out the night.

MORE THAN ONCE I THOUGHT: I MIGHT AS WELL BE DEAD.

We were the last to leave. I can't tell you the exact time we walked out of there, but the sun was just coming up. All night and into the morning, we drank, snorted cocaine and took other drugs, maybe even some Ecstasy. I don't remember much through the haze of intoxicants, narcotics and hallucinogens, but I do have a short mental video loop of a part of that night, which still haunts me to this day. I'm walking through clubs, the studio and on the streets of Hollywood. All the people I see have glazed looks on their faces. Their eyes are like glass. They seem soulless and mindless, like zombies. The scariest part of these running mental images is that I look just like them. I'd become a zombie too.

My housemate and I wanted to go home after leaving the studio, but there were no taxis to be found and we were in no shape to walk. Drunk and delirious, we stumbled from block to block for an hour or two, trying to find a cab. The only traffic seemed to be school buses loaded with clean-cut, laughing kids, which seemed all the more surreal given our wasted state and paranoid feelings.

Wading through the streams of boys and girls carrying their SpongeBob Square Pants book bags and Hello Kitty backpacks, we were like two stoners who'd wandered into Pleasantville. The kids looked at us with disdain and fear. I swear if they'd had parent-issued pepper-sprayers, they would've used them when they saw us coming.

I was just hoping they didn't recognize me and scream, "It's Nick Carter from the Backstreet Boys!!" The thought of being spotted like that made my stomach turn. I didn't feel worthy of our fans at that moment. I was disgusted with myself for being in that condition at an hour when normal, sane people were beginning their productive days. My self-loathing only worsened when we tried to board a city bus. The driver took one look at us two burnouts on the sidewalk and slammed the door in our faces.

THEY SEEM SOULLESS AND MINDLESS, LIKE ZOMBIES.

Too messed up to board the Metro bus? This was definitely a new low. Finally we found a cab and rode to our house in Hollywood. We'd only lived in this place for a week so there was barely any furniture or food. I tried to sleep, but my head was spinning and my stomach was churning. I freaked out and went to the kitchen in search of something to relieve my bellyache. Realizing I hadn't eaten since lunch the day before, I found some cream of mushroom soup and tried to prepare it. Making something as simple as soup seemed more complicated in that state than making a five-course meal while sober.

My housemate stumbled into the kitchen. He couldn't sleep either. He seemed to be feeling like old dirt too. We walked around each other without exchanging a word. We were so zoned out it was eerie. Later, he told me that he also felt sick to his stomach at the same time, as he was starving. We both had this sense that we desperately needed food just to make it through another minute.

I managed to heat up the soup and force it down my throat. My stomach felt better after I ate, but my head was pounding as if screaming "Code Blue, Code Blue!" It felt like some evil creature had invaded my body and was busy hammering on my brain. Blind with pain, I stumbled back to my bedroom, praying that I'd pass out before the clamor grew worse. I made the mistake of looking in a mirror on the way to bed. The guy I saw there was a very scary stranger.

My face looked bloated, the way it would appear in a carnival fun house mirror. My body was twice its normal width due to the 50 pounds I'd gained from hard drinking, overeating and lack of exercise. My skin was ashen gray trending toward translucent. My eyes were puffy and blood red. I'd aged a thousand years. I *did* look like a zombie—like my great-grandfather's ghost.

The thought hit me: *I don't know who I am anymore.* Then the panic set in. *This is not me. This is not who I am or who I want to be. I deserve better. I can be better than this.*

I had never been in such frightening shape emotionally, mentally or physically. I was scared for my life. My body seemed to be crashing and my brain was close behind.

I found my cell phone and called my publicist.

"I need to check into rehab. Will you take me?"

BINGING TO OBLIVION

When you binge drink, it's as if this thick cloud fills your head. I did things that I would never do in my right mind. I'd been on a long stretch of all-nighters and the body count of dead brain cells was racking up. I was doing crazy, spontaneous, impulsive things with no thought to the consequences. When friends or family members called me out, my pat response was "It is what it is" or "That's just life."

THE THOUGHT HIT ME: I DON'T KNOW WHO I AM ANYMORE.

I wasn't facing my demons; I was dancing with them. No wonder the people who cared about me were throwing their hands up in the air. *Note to self*: When those who truly care about you and have your best interests at heart are waving red flags in your face, screaming "Stop!" and talking about an intervention, maybe, just maybe, you really are standing on the edge of the abyss.

The irony was that while I ignored or argued with people who were trying to help me avoid a total meltdown, I'd become totally paranoid about other perceived threats because of my chronic substance abuse. More than once I canceled airline flights at the last minute because I had visions of crashing. On a couple of occasions, I had already been on the plane when panic overcame me and I ran out before the attendants closed the cabin door, leaving my bags to make the trip without me. Everyone had some qualms about flying after the 9/11 terrorist attacks, but my paranoia took me to the outer reaches of sanity. At one point, I actually looked into buying a remote lodge in Canada to hide out in, I was so sure that the world was headed for chaos.

I WASN'T FACING MY DEMONS; I WAS DANCING WITH THEM.

I'm certain that some people were amused by my erratic behavior, but it was a really serious matter. My therapist and I have talked about this period at length. I see now that the drugs and alcohol in my system had altered my brain chemistry so much that I wasn't thinking or acting like myself. I truly was a stranger. My personality had been lost to all the toxins in my system. I wasn't who I was meant to be.

I may have told myself and others that I was just making up for lost time because I'd worked so hard when I was younger, but the hard truth is that I'd used my *lost teen years* as an excuse to abandon all personal responsibility and self-control.

DISABLERS

I now take full responsibility for my behavior during this very ugly period of my life. One of the biggest mistakes I made at that time was surrounding myself with enablers, or, more accurately, *dis*-ablers. They may have been enablers in the sense that they were binge drinkers and drug users who partied around the clock and encouraged me to do the same, but they were also disablers because running with them only brought out the worst in me. Bear in mind that disablers are not to be blamed as *I* let all that happen, no doubt about it. Disablers are, however, to be avoided.

I realized after lots of reflection that I was afraid of being alone with my demons. Surrounding myself with other binge drinkers and drug users made me feel better about getting wasted night after night. I didn't want to be alone or with people who questioned my self-destructive behavior. I was afraid of that, even though I knew in my heart that true friends want you to be at your best, not your worst. The people who really care about you will get in your face and tell you when you are headed for a crash and burn. True friends enable you by helping you build upon your strengths instead of encouraging you to give in to your weaknesses.

When I was in the binge-and-bump mode, I chose to ignore the warning signs I saw nearly every night, but those signs seared themselves into my brain as if my subconscious was persisting in its efforts to get the message through. I remember, night after night, going to the bars and clubs with my group of friends and seeing people who made me fear for the future if I didn't change my ways.

TRUE FRIENDS ENABLE YOU BY HELPING YOU BUILD UPON YOUR STRENGTHS...

There was this crowd of *old zombies* in their fifties and sixties who had never given up the lifestyle of hard drinking and drugging. Some members of our crowd were friendly with them, as if they were members of the same club, but I was ambiguous.

More than once, I looked at them and thought, *That's me. I'm going to be hanging in these same clubs thirty years from now and life is just going to pass me by.*

Still, I didn't turn and walk out when I had those thoughts. I was afraid to face the truth about myself as reflected in their faces and bodies so ravaged by alcoholism and drug abuse. Misery really does love company. I didn't want to hang out with clean-living people because they would have made me feel guilty and stupid, but the disablers helped me convince myself that everyone was into drugs and binge drinking. We told ourselves we were party animals living the good life. It was all a lie. People who are doing drugs may claim they are having fun, but in their hearts they are anguished, dejected, sad human beings. They are lost and they don't know how to find themselves.

If you are on that same track right now, please let me help you. Don't wait for things to change. You have to change first. I am sharing stories to help you see the reality of your situation. I don't want you to ever experience the horror yourself. I'm your best example of a bad example. Don't follow me. Follow my warnings.

Sooner or later we all have to face our demons or they will destroy us. Looking into the mirror, I saw the depleted and tormented shell of the man I'd become and vowed to reclaim the man I wanted to be. I am still in that fight. Some days I win. Other days, I fall short.

YOU HAVE TO CHANGE FIRST.

It's not easy, but every day that I'm fighting for my life is far better than the agony of spending another night amongst the zombies. You will feel the same, although I hope you never fall as far as I did.

Did I mention that I became a heavy smoker during this time too? We all know there is nothing better for a professional singer than cigarettes! Have you ever read the medical reports on the combined effects of heavy drinking and heavy smoking? Or binge drinking? Very scary stuff.

I hope it's clear from my experience that there is nothing cool about this stuff. I'm not proud of any of it. I cringe when I write about it and find myself afraid to this day that I may have put my physical and mental health at risk. I did not deal with my demons for a long time and I've paid a price. But one of the scariest things is that I still don't know what that full price may be because there can be severe long-term damage from all the things I did to my body.

During this time, I clearly let my many issues, fears and emotions drive my actions when I should have taken control. Even when I felt myself falling at full speed, and my friends and family were sounding the alarms, I still refused to face those demons head-on. I hid from them by drinking, doing drugs and smoking.

If you have similar demons, you might be more inclined to deal with them if you understand what binge drinking, illegal drug use, smoking and similar addictive and self-destructive behavior can actually do to you. A critical step in my own effort to create a better life was to commit to educating myself as much as possible. I stopped living as if I didn't care about the future. Instead of ignoring or downplaying the warnings others raised, I began investigating them to see if there was any credence to them. What I learned helped scare me into looking for a better way. Maybe it will help you too.

'TILL DEATH DO WE PARTY

When I think back to my binge drinking and drug-using days, I see a contradiction that never occurred to me then. I used to look at the old zombies in the bars and clubs as alcoholics and addicts. Yet the truth was that my friends and I were drinking much more and doing many more drugs than most of them. We didn't think of ourselves as alcoholics or addicts. We thought we were just "partying."

I STOPPED LIVING AS IF I DIDN'T CARE ABOUT THE FUTURE.

We were in denial, obviously. The fact is that our bodies didn't know the difference between *just partying* and serious addiction. Our livers, brains, kidneys and hearts were suffering from just as much damage as the vital organs in those older bar flies and die-hard clubbers.

You can pretend you don't have demons. You can think of yourself as young and bulletproof, or as someone *just having fun*. But sooner or later, your body will speak the truth, and you will crash and burn. Or worse, you'll hurt someone else.

Like most binge drinkers, I rationalized my heavy drinking by saying I didn't do it every day, or I never did it before six o' clock at night. I also convinced myself that I could stop any time I wanted to. But when my therapist talked to me about my drinking, he asked how I'd feel if I killed someone by driving drunk, or what if my young fans saw me wasted on the streets some night? What if I was kicked out of Backstreet for being a drunk?

The truth is, you can hide from the demons, but you can't hide from the consequences. If you are acting like the king or queen of denial when it comes to binge drinking or drug abuse, you certainly aren't alone. My friends and I were there and so are many other people of all ages and economic levels. I've seen reports that indicate nearly nineteen percent of those between the ages of 12 and 20 have tried binge drinking and a CDC survey found that as many as one quarter of all high school students and adults between the ages of 18 and 35 have done it.

Experts say that more than thirty million adults binge drink now, and that number isn't decreasing. I was also surprised to learn that more than forty thousand people die each year in the United States because of it—that's half of all alcohol-related deaths in the country. Medical reports say that not all binge drinkers are alcoholics, though most have serious alcohol abuse problems.

The toll is steep. One study reported that those who binge drink are fourteen times more likely to drive while intoxicated than moderate drinkers. Approximately five thousand young people under the legal drinking age die from alcohol-related causes each year, but those are just the easy stats to collect. Who knows how many people die prematurely because of the damage they've done to their bodies and minds from alcohol and drug abuse?

Medical research has found evidence that binge drinking can affect the development of brains in teenagers, whose bodies typically haven't reached full maturity yet. According to one study, binge-drinking teens may actually suffer a loss of white matter in their brains, which is the tissue that affects learning and controls communication.

Drinking until you drop is a huge trend on college campuses in particular, but it's happening off campus too. I've heard that there are concerns about an increase in binge drinking among women with children. I read a few years ago about a woman who killed herself and seven others in a head-on collision while driving the wrong-way on a highway in New York State. She was en route home from a camping trip with five children in the car including her son, daughter and three nieces all under the age of nine. Police found a bottle of vodka in the car and subsequent tests showed that she'd had the equivalent of ten drinks in her system and that she'd been smoking marijuana too.

It's one thing to endanger your own life with reckless drinking and drug use, but can you imagine killing your own children, loved ones and other innocent people?

BINGE AND A BUMP

As I mentioned earlier, my friends and I would often take a hit of cocaine late in the night so we could keep partying. It's a pretty common practice among the clubbing set especially.

At the time, I thought feeling more awake and pumped up was a good idea, but I later found out that when you drink heavily and then do cocaine on top of it, some weird and dangerous reactions occur in the body. For one thing, cocaine is a stimulant that sends alcohol more quickly to the brain, so if you've been binge drinking, cocaine will make you drunker faster. Worse than that, the mix of alcohol and coke in your liver can create a toxic chemical called cocaethylene. This chemical is even nastier than it sounds. I'm told it is the only known example of the body creating a third drug after you've taken two others. Along with damaging your liver, cocaethylene may also cause serious heart problems or even heart attack.

When I started looking into this for reasons I'll explain later, I also discovered that there are some potentially serious dangers to drinking while using many prescription drugs, too; especially depressants because the combination increases the depressant effects of alcohol. Adderall, an amphetamine used to treat ADD and other disorders and often taken by college students to help them focus while studying, should never be mixed with alcohol, nor should sleep medications for obvious reasons. Even aspirin, antihistamines, ibuprofen and acetaminophen can cause problems to your liver or stomach if you drink with them in your system.

My research into all of the dangers of mixing alcohol and drugs came only after I'd abused my own body and mind for years by drinking and taking whatever drug was offered. I never thought of my binge drinking and drug use as an addiction, but in many ways, I was an addict. Acknowledging that I wasn't just a fun-loving party guy, but someone with a serious problem, was a really tough but necessary step toward changing my life.

In my heart and mind, I knew that there was something more to my heavy drinking and drug use than simply wanting to have a good time with my buddies. I was afraid to ask myself what the real reason was because

I didn't want to deal with that demon. My therapist helped me understand that you can't change your life for the better if you refuse to honestly look at what drives your self-destructive behavior. Sooner or later, you have to ask, "Why am I doing this?" Am I really just looking for a good time or am I self-medicating so I don't have to face my fears? Is this the only way I can deal with the pain? The depression? The emptiness in my life?

I'D GET ANTSY AND LONELY AND THE DEMONS WOULD COME OUT TO TAUNT ME.

Like many people who abuse drugs and alcohol, I pretended that passing out or getting sick night after night was no big deal. *Everyone else was doing it*, I thought. I certainly had friends who were much bigger drinkers and drug users than I was. Of course, I was playing the denial game, trying to convince myself and everyone else that I was in control and that my behavior was perfectly normal. Some people can snap themselves out of that self-delusional pattern in one of their more lucid, sober moments. Others need the help of friends, family or professionals. I encourage you to do whatever works for you, but urge you to do it before it's too late.

Eventually I realized that rather than trying to *break* self-destructive behavioral patterns, it's much easier to replace them with more constructive activities. Instead of going drinking every night, for example, I began working out, reading motivational books, and focusing on expanding my mind and building up my body. My therapist helped me learn that replacing the highs of heavy drinking and drug use with the much longer-lasting highs of a good work out or self-education would take a lot of the stress and anxieties out of my life.

Part of my problem was that my career led to a lifestyle where I had long periods of intense activity including touring, recording and traveling, followed by long periods with much more idle time on my hands. I didn't know what to do with myself during the slower times on the road or at home. I'd get antsy and lonely and the demons would come out to taunt me. To hide from them, I'd call up my drinking buddies and hit the bars.

Finding other ways to spend my free time was a big step in the right direction. I began using that time to explore new career opportunities, healthier lifestyles, and new subjects that had intrigued me.

PROMISES TO KEEP

I didn't discover these methods for breaking my addiction to binge drinking and drugs until I committed to changing my life. Because I had no idea where to start, I figured I'd ask for some help.

That first step, when I called my publicist to accompany me to rehab, wasn't an easy one to take. I remember sitting and crying in my car for what seemed like hours before driving to get her. We then drove to Promises, an addiction treatment center in a big, old craftsman-style house in West L.A.

I WAS IN A TRANCE
AS WE WALKED IN.

I was in a trance as we walked in. My publicist explained that I was still under the influence of alcohol and cocaine, and maybe Ecstasy too. The admissions person calmly asked me a series of questions as if this was a normal thing—having a totally wasted boy-band singer walk in blitzed and scared out of his mind.

While I was being given a tour of the place, I recognized other celebrities in residence. Some of them tried to hide their faces. Others looked at me like, "It's about time you checked in."

Seeing them made the reality of my situation hit all the harder. Promises was obviously a well-run, comfortable place, but I wasn't sure if it was for me. I wasn't much for structured environments like this. It felt too confining. *Maybe I needed to do this on my own*, I thought.

I told the Promises staff member that I wanted to go home and think about the residential program. He suggested that I begin my treatment as an outpatient patient, which would allow me to come back for counseling and therapy. Really, I'd decided that before anyone else could help me, I needed to get my mind cleansed and my thinking straightened out. The only way I could see doing that was to remove myself from the poisoned environment I'd been living in.

IT FELT TOO CONFINING.

Then the thought hit me: *Cool Springs. I need to go back to Cool Springs.*

PERSONAL NOTES

CHAPTER SIX

COOL SPRINGS REHAB

I WAS A wreck during the recording of Backstreet's *Unbreakable* album in 2006. I knew I was seriously mistreating my body and that I wasn't living up to my true potential.

I was so depressed that I couldn't contribute a lot to the songwriting process or do much else on the album aside from singing in the studio. I was in a steep downward spiral, dealing with problems clearly of my own making.

AS MUCH AS I LONGED TO MAKE A CHANGE, I DIDN'T KNOW WHAT LIFE WOULD BE LIKE IF I GAVE UP MY DEPENDENCIES.

I wanted to stop partying and getting wasted, but I was afraid to. As much as I longed to make a change, I didn't know what life would be like if I gave up my dependencies. I was like a guy who freezes halfway up while climbing a wall. I knew I had to make a move, but I was afraid to let go long enough to reach higher.

Fear of the unknown can hold you back; so if you ever find yourself locked up like that, knowing that you need to make a change but afraid to pursue something better, ask yourself: *What's the worst that could happen?* Then consider: *Is it better or worse than where you are now?* Sometimes we subconsciously equate change with death. We're afraid that if we fail or fall short, something in us will die. But in most cases, when you let go to reach for something better, you actually improve your situation.

I was trapped in a self-destructive lifestyle. I knew I needed to break free. Thoughts of escape kept coming to me, though I felt more like I needed to run toward something better. Your life is the product of the decisions you make along the way, and my decisions had been consistently bad for a long stretch in my twenties.

I WAS LIKE A GUY WHO FREEZES HALFWAY UP WHILE CLIMBING A WALL.

Have you ever felt like you weren't the person you wanted to be, or the person you were meant to be? In my case, things just seemed out of synch (no reference to that other boy band intended!). I was lucky to have my music and BSB because other than that, I was lost. My relationships with my family members weren't going well and I hadn't found a girlfriend yet who seemed interested in anything other than my celebrity status, which I never felt particularly comfortable with myself.

My therapist later taught me about the concepts of the *authentic self* and the *inner critic*. Basically, whether we know it or not, most of us have certain principles and values that make up the moral code by which we live. These values include ideas about what is right and wrong, good and bad, proper and improper. Most of these are based in common sense standards that society in general views as good for our shared quality of life. Few would argue, for example, that honesty is usually the best policy, that fairness is better than selfishness, and that it's best to treat other people like you would want to be treated.

We live consciously and subconsciously according to the moral code that we've created for ourselves based on how we grew up and what we've learned along the way. If you were lucky enough to have parents, teachers, spiritual leaders, or other adults who guided you and worked to instill strong values within you, then you likely are very conscious of those values when you make decisions.

My parents weren't big on instilling such values in us—at least not intentionally. They did provide us with some good examples of hard work, but they never talked about other values, principles or moral codes, as I mentioned earlier. Since my formal education ended at such a young age, I didn't get much help in that department from teachers or coaches either.

Still, over the years, I did develop my own set of principles. I didn't always live by them, but I used them to measure my own behavior and the behavior of people I met. I came to appreciate traits like honesty, excellence, continuous growth and trustworthiness.

INTERIOR WARNING SYSTEM

I sincerely wanted to live according to those values, but as I entered my mid-twenties, I sensed that I'd turned my back on many of them. It felt as though my life had come off the tracks. I didn't much like or respect myself. If you ever have feelings like that, my advice is to pay attention to them. Our survival instincts are strong, but sometimes we tend to ignore them. We get busy or comfortable or scared. Change can be frightening, but when your instincts are screaming for you to save yourself, the prospect of not making a change can be the scariest thing of all.

IT FELT AS THOUGH MY LIFE HAD COME OFF THE TRACKS.

When we work in the recording studio, we put in long and often intense hours, but there's also lots of time spent waiting for the studio engineers to perform their magic. Downtime was my downfall. In our free hours I was constantly partying, going out to clubs every night and often hitting the bars during the day. I was surrounded by an entourage of people addicted to the same party mentality. Our binges kept getting worse and worse, lasting until three or four in the morning when we'd end the night in the homes of strangers. We'd be obliterated to the point where we'd wake up the next morning not knowing where we were or how we'd gotten there.

The only time I felt good during that stretch was when we moved our recording sessions to Sound Kitchen Studios, just south of Nashville in an area known as Cool Springs. While the name Cool Springs might conjure images of a backwater town, that was not the case. There is a big Galleria mall there surrounded by shops and restaurants. Beyond those shops, in the town of Franklin, there are hilly, wooded neighborhoods with nice, comfortable homes.

The area reminded me of the times I spent with my Grandpa Carter, who was from Chattanooga—a beautiful part of Tennessee. He later moved to Jamestown, NY, and when we lived in Florida, we would drive from Tampa up through Tennessee on our way to visit him and my grandma. These trips provided some of my few cherished memories of childhood. Dad would pile all of us into a van, and for me the best part of the trek was driving through the mountains in Grandpa's home state. I was fascinated by the Tennessee countryside, which was much more dramatic than anything I'd seen in Florida. I felt as though there was something healing about that part of the country.

It's probably no coincidence that I was drawn to Tennessee and ended up buying a home there for myself when I got older. Since I've mostly lived in urban or heavy residential areas, I find it comforting to be in a more rural setting at times. I like the slower pace, the normalcy and the family feel of Cool Springs. For all of these reasons I felt better there, but my friends in the area were a major factor too.

We were staying at a hotel near the studio so I really didn't explore the area much until I had an opportunity to hang out with Andrew Fromm, a great songwriter who had two songs on our *Millennium* album. We were working at Sound Kitchen Studios with him and Dan Muckala, another award-winning songwriter and producer, when Andrew invited me to the nearby house he'd just moved into after coming to the Nashville area.

Andrew is this Jewish guy from New Jersey who moved to Tennessee and discovered that he loves the country life. He drove me to his new place in Cool Springs, which spans two adjoining Nashville suburbs, Brentwood and Franklin. He was real proud of his home and excited about settling down in such a laid back area with so many creative and talented musicians. He is a very grounded, clean-living guy who doesn't drink or do drugs. Back then,

Andrew was single, but now he has a beautiful wife and son.

Being around such positive and healthy people was a big change for me. I felt like I could relax and breathe around them. Their idea of partying was nothing like the Hollywood crowd's. We weren't in Cool Springs that long, but I found myself thinking several times during our stay that it might be nice to have my own place there someday, just to get away from the craziness of life on the road or in L.A.

GOIN' COUNTRY

Cool Springs came to mind again after I had my Night of the Zombies crash and burn. When I walked out of Promises rehab center in Los Angeles, I knew that I needed to get away from the whole 24/7 Hollywood party scene. I wanted to clean up my act, but it was evident there'd be no chance of doing that if I stayed around people who partied all the time.

I FELT LIKE I COULD RELAX AND BREATHE AROUND THEM.

The more I thought about it, the more I liked the idea of heading to Tennessee. Cool Springs and the town of Franklin seemed perfect because there's a big music scene and my friends there were better influences on me. I knew they wouldn't be pushing me to go out night after night. I envied their lives in many ways because they seemed so content and grounded. So, I headed to the hills of Tennessee to find the person I wanted to be.

Some of my L.A. friends saw it as moving *to the backwoods* and thought it was a random thing for me to do, but I had a plan. After hitting bottom in L.A., I went to the country and bought a place that I jokingly referred to as *my refuge in the middle of nowhere*. Honestly, mine is probably the ugliest house you can find in my very nice little neighborhood. You would never expect a celebrity to live there.

It's a brick, two-story home that looks in some ways like the *Amityville Horror* house—as if it could be haunted, even though it was brand new when I moved in.

I still go there for its serenity. It's become sort of a cool getaway for my friends and me. The fact that it looks like a normal house is really appealing. Even when I'm away from Tennessee, I feel comforted just knowing that place is there. You might say that I take Cool Springs with me wherever I go. It's not like I load up the house, but I do carry that sense of peace and contemplation with me. I've learned that you can make a home within yourself. No matter where I am, I can go to Cool Springs mentally whenever I need to relax, calm myself and heal.

Fate must have taken me to Cool Springs because my home there turned out to be the perfect place to escape what had become a very negative environment. There, I was able to focus on moving my life in a more positive direction. Sometimes change is good. Sometimes it is absolutely necessary. In so many ways my Tennessee home served as my rehab center.

MIND-OPENING GIFT

I knew deep down inside that if I kept running around with my partying friends, I was headed for a breakdown, prison, early grave, or something worse. The people I hung out with in Cool Springs were just more positive. Their interests were geared toward music, their families and their faith. They didn't lecture me or try to convert me. They just inspired me by their basic goodness.

YOU MIGHT SAY THAT I TAKE COOL SPRINGS WITH ME WHEREVER I GO.

Looking back, I couldn't say that Andrew Fromm and his crowd saved my life exactly, but they did introduce me to a much healthier lifestyle. They helped me to take the first steps toward changing my self-destructive patterns of behavior. The path they walk is just so much better for me. Isn't it crazy how the choices we make can have such an impact on our lives? As much as I resisted change, my life became so much better when I finally moved out of a bad environment into a much better one. It's as if I went from the darkness into the light.

The other majorly positive influence in my whole Cool Springs rehab experience was the book that Kevin Richardson had given me on my 21st birthday. For several years it just sat on the shelves in different apartments or homes as I moved from place to place. I packed it up and took it wherever I lived, but I never read it. Then, after I'd moved to Cool Springs and had some time for introspection, my eyes wandered to that book on a shelf and, for the first time, I pulled it down and began reading it.

The book is *Why Some Positive Thinkers Get Powerful Results* written by Norman Vincent Peale, a minister and inspirational speaker. I know what you're saying: *A self-help book? Right! C'mon Nick, are you 100 years old or what?* Tease me all you want, I can take it. This book changed my life because it helped me change my way of thinking. Its simple message—that a more positive attitude can lead to a better life—flipped a switch and turned on the lights.

I WAS WINGING LIFE, MORE OR LESS, WITHOUT ANY REAL DIRECTION, GOALS, OR PLANS.

I'm not saying this book is the secret to success, happiness and a life without worries. But as my first self-help book, it was an introduction to new ways of looking at things, and it inspired me to go deeper in my reading and reflections. Kevin's gift really helped me move away from being a self-destructive *victim*.

Just as the Cool Springs house moved me physically to a healthier environment, Peale's book moved me mentally into a healthier way of thinking. Because I was so young when BSB took off, I never spent any time planning or setting goals for my life. I didn't have to. Once we had a hit record, I had more money than I'd ever dreamed of making. What I did each and every day was pretty much determined by the group's schedule for writing, recording and performing. I just went with the flow. There wasn't much down time, which was a good thing because that's when I tended to get out of control with my partying as you now know.

I was winging life, more or less, without any real direction, goals, or plans. And because of the way I grew up, I had a lot of built-up anger, hurt and insecurity that I didn't know how to unload. In his day, Norman Vincent Peale was like a combination of the Rev. Billy Graham and Dr. Phil. He was a minister and a master of self-help. His books sold millions and millions of copies, though he had his critics too. Most of his detractors said his message was too simple, but simple was what I needed at that point.

I devoured that book, which is basically a bunch of stories about people who've overcome problems and challenges, along with tips about setting goals and going after them, dealing with depression and negative thoughts, kicking bad habits and motivating yourself. It's sort of an old-fashioned book, but it encouraged me to read more modern and more scientific books on things like *emotional intelligence*, *learned optimism*, and *life strategies*.

MAN WITH A PLAN

This may all sound like self-help bull to you, but I can only tell you what worked for me. It's easy to be sarcastic and critical, yet much more difficult to admit that sometimes we just don't know what we don't know. Up until that point, I'd always believed that self-help books were for other people. I thought I had everything I needed—career success, fame, and money. Then, I found myself at the bottom of that deep, dark, gaping black hole I've talked so much about, looking up and wondering how the heck I got there.

I DIDN'T KNOW WHAT I DIDN'T KNOW UNTIL I OPENED MY MIND TO THE FACT THAT MAYBE I NEEDED MORE HELP THAN I'D THOUGHT.

I didn't know what I didn't know until I opened my mind to the fact that maybe I needed more help than I'd thought. When I finally read the book Kevin gave me, I realized in my heart and mind that something had to change or I was going to destroy my career and my health, and maybe take some innocent people down with me. My instincts told me to get away from friends who only brought out the worst in me, and to go somewhere that wasn't full of temptations and distractions. Once I got to Cool Springs, though, I really didn't have a clue what to do next.

Until I read Peale's book, I had no plan. Worse than that, I didn't know I needed one. I also knew nothing about creating a plan. So, I was about as helpless as a baby when it came to *rehabbing* myself. I am not asking anyone to feel sorry for me; I had a great career. I had friends. I had money. I had no problem getting a date.

I DIDN'T FEEL WORTHY OF
TRUST AND AFFECTION.

What I didn't have was peace of mind, true happiness, self-respect, self-approval, self-love, self-confidence, or much hope for the future.

I didn't feel worthy of trust and affection. And I was tired of feeling that way. I wanted something better, so I had to *be* better. That much, I figured out. So, I went to work on my body, mind and spirit.

I approached my rehabilitation in a very uncharacteristic fashion. I was very meticulous and methodical. I even compartmentalized. I thought of every room in the house as a section of my brain that needed work. I won't bore you with the details other than to say that I saw each room as the storage place for certain negative thoughts, memories, habits, addictions, and resentments. I went from one room to the next cleaning out the cobwebs and dust bunnies, throwing out the garbage, turning on the lights, and opening the windows to let in fresh air.

As I did that physically in every room of the house, I did the same things mentally and emotionally inside my head. After I moved in and read Peale's book, I went to work organizing my surroundings and my *inner self.* I straightened up things both literally and figuratively.

My brother and sisters and various roommates will tell you I'd always been a messy person as far as housekeeping was concerned, and in general life too. I wanted to change in both departments. One of my goals was to think and act with a clearer head, so I made that part of my conscious process.

From my readings I'd learned the value of setting goals, writing them down to reinforce them and following a step-by-step plan to pursue them.

I took that seriously. I even went to the office supply store one day and got a big white board on a stand like you see in corporate meeting rooms. I bought some markers and scribbled down all of the goals I could think of.

I'd done something similar a few years earlier and saw how effectively it could work. At the time, I was trying to stop smoking. I knew smoking causes cancer and destroys your lungs. Everybody knows that. Yet, like so many people, I just couldn't seem to get my act together long enough to quit. It was a habit. An addiction, really, and I didn't have the willpower to break it until I tried something a little crazy. I finally went into my closet one day, pulled out a white t-shirt, grabbed a marker and wrote on the t-shirt, "I do not like smoking. This is not me!"

I then wore that t-shirt to bed every night for about three months, reading the anti-smoking message on it before I fell asleep and then again first thing in the morning when I woke up, and I just stopped smoking that way. That's the power of the human brain!

You really can program your brain to get you what you want. That's my belief. I've read a lot about this and there are many who say that if you set goals, write them down, work on them every day and ask for the help of whatever higher power you believe in, you can achieve them.

One of my favorite sayings along this line is that you should shoot for the moon because even if you miss, you will land among the stars. I like that because it reminds me that when you dare to dream for better things and you pursue them, even if you don't get exactly what you'd hoped for, you still end up better than you were without dreams.

YOU REALLY CAN PROGRAM YOUR BRAIN TO GET YOU WHAT YOU WANT.

GO FOR THE GOAL

Goal setting is imperative. It is so important to have goals that you can envision actually happening without the help of magic, a huge gift from Oprah, or a body swap with Richard Branson. Visualization is really important, too.

I try to imagine myself moving toward a goal step by step, then accomplishing that goal and truly feeling what it is like to achieve it. When you do that, you imprint both the process and the joy you'll experience onto your subconscious. I believe your mind then goes to work on helping you attain your goal, making it seem as if you've already been there before. You won't be as intimidated because the path will seem familiar.

I HAVE TO BE ABLE TO VISUALIZE AND THEN TAKE THE STEPS NECESSARY TO ACHIEVE A GOAL.

Once I learned about the principle of visualization, I adopted it with a passion. I'd been one of those people who lived on a whim. I'd change directions depending on which way the wind was blowing, or whom I was hanging out with. I fought changes, even positive ones, and I wanted to stick with bad habits even when I knew they were bad because I preferred what was familiar to what was unfamiliar.

Setting goals takes you out of that mindset and puts your brain in forward gear. Instead of being in park, you are in drive. It's so important to have goals because if you don't know where you want to go, how will you ever get there? Maybe you believe that where you are right now is where you are supposed to be and where you'll always be. Now that's fine if you are happy and fulfilled, but if you aren't, then what the heck are you thinking? Are there chains on your feet or bars on the walls? If there aren't, then you have the power to choose a better life and the power to go after it.

BREAKING IT DOWN

Deciding to set goals is a good first step, but if you are busy and easily distracted like me, you have to get very detailed in defining those goals, writing them down and setting a timeframe for accomplishing them. I have to set goals in a way that allows me to immediately act on them, even if it's just taking really small steps, so I feel right away that I'm making progress.

It would never work for me just to say my goal is to turn my life around. That's a great long-term, overall goal but how do you get there? What do you have to do? Those questions can seem daunting at first, so it might help you to think of goals as part of the song of your life. You create your goals just as you would write that song. Here, let me explain:

Songwriters typically have a vision or theme in mind when they begin a song. Then they write it note-by-note, word-by-word. In the same way, you may have a vision of the life you want to create. You can string a series of smaller goals together to create that life, just as songwriters string verses together to create their songs. I have to be able to visualize and then take the steps necessary to achieve a goal. To turn my life around, some of the step-by-step goals I needed to accomplish were to lose weight and get back in good physical condition, to stop binge drinking and doing illegal drugs, to remove myself from unhealthy environments, to find more positive and encouraging friends, and to become more engaged in creating music for myself and the group.

Once I had those more specific goals outlined, I went even further in breaking them down so I could gauge my progress easily. For example, I gave myself a couple of months to lose ten pounds as a starter toward getting healthier, though my longer-term goal was fifty pounds! I figured that I'd just keep a scale handy so I could measure my progress pound by pound.

I'd already removed myself from the binge-drinking and bar-hopping crowd by changing my environment and chilling in Cool Springs. There, I was surrounded by people like Andrew Fromm and Dan Muckala, who were much more interested in making great music than getting wasted night after night. I kept beer and all other alcohol out of my Tennessee house and stocked up on healthy fruits and vegetables.

You'll notice that my goals weren't pie-in-the-sky things. I wasn't trying to become Mr. Universe; I was just working to get back in better shape so I didn't look like a slob on stage or in photo shoots. Writing more of my own music was also a goal within my reach, though it required more focus and effort than I'd been putting in for a couple of years. If I'd set the goal of writing a rock opera or a concerto it might have been a stretch. The idea is that you should dare to dream big, but be realistic in setting goals so you can accomplish them within a reasonable amount of time.

Once you have some momentum going, you can raise the bar higher and higher as you move forward.

Make sure your goals are things you have some control over. Winning the lottery is definitely not a goal that you can achieve on your own, but finishing a local marathon race, losing twenty-five pounds, or continuing your education are all goals that are within reach and don't necessarily require superhuman powers.

Once you've chosen achievable goals within your control and reach, the next step is to come up with a plan of action. My advice is to put together a daily calendar in which you list the positive steps toward attaining each goal that you can take every day.

MAKE SURE YOUR GOALS ARE THINGS YOU HAVE SOME CONTROL OVER.

Many well-intentioned goals are forgotten or neglected because their equally well-intentioned goal-setters get caught up in their jobs or personal lives. I know it's tempting to think *I'll work on that goal tomorrow or next week*, but don't procrastinate. Do the opposite. What would that be called by the way? *Concrastinate?* Whatever, as the real-life Benjamin on your dollars once said, "Don't put off until tomorrow what you can do today."

Set up a daily goal-workout program, just like you'd follow a workout routine at the gym. Do something every day in some measureable way to move closer to your goals. It might help you to create a program of small daily steps that lead you to bigger weekly steps that lead you, over a specific period of time, to finally accomplishing your goal.

One final step in this goal-achieving process is to find at least one coach-cheerleader-encourager with whom you can share your goals, plan and timeline. This should be a person you trust, someone who wants to see you succeed in building a better life. So, don't pick your worst enemy, or a rival, or the bar owner who was getting rich off your binge drinking habit.

Another thing I learned from my reading is that some people have a scarcity mentality. They think of success as a limited commodity, like a pie with only so many pieces. People with this mentality are likely to think that if you succeed, then there is less chance for them to find success. Stay away from them. They will not support you and they may even try to sabotage you.

Look instead for people with an abundance mentality. These people see success as an unlimited commodity, like stars in the universe. They want you to succeed because they think there is enough success and happiness in the universe for everyone to claim a heaping helping. Sign these people up for your team whenever you find them. Share your dreams and goals with them and support them just as they will support you.

BE YOUR OWN BEST FRIEND

In truth, the only thing that can hold you back is that person in the mirror staring back at you. I am not just saying that. I lived it. For way too long, I didn't think I was worthy of a better life so even when great things happened to me, I didn't allow myself to enjoy them or to feel grateful for them. What we tend to forget is that, as far as anyone knows, this is our one brief shot at a life. It doesn't last forever. It can end before you know it. Why not sing while you are on stage? Why not give it all you've got? Why not use up every ounce of your talent and energy and make the most of every minute?

It helped me to first think about where I wanted to end up in life and then think about how I wanted to get there. Some life coaches have their clients write down what they want people to say about them at their own funerals. The idea is to begin with the end in mind, meaning you first imagine the qualities and reputation you want to have by the end of your life, then you do all you can to be that person. I can see the value in that approach but it's a little dark for me. Another approach that I actually prefer and actively use, is to write down goals as if they've already been reached. It's a way of programming your subconscious mind much like you would program a computer.

If you are comfortable just the way you are and it's working for you, that's fine. But if you want to change and create a better life, goal setting is a great way to do that. I've done a lot of research on the best way to achieve your goals and I've learned that when you write them down as if they've already been reached, you imprint them in your subconscious. It's very similar to what happens when you practice visualization. This seems to help make my goals more realistic and achievable and it also boosts my confidence.

THE MORE I THINK ABOUT MY GOALS, THE MORE I OWN THEM.

For this method to be even more effective, it helps to repeat your goals on a regular basis. The more I think about my goals, the more I own them. There have been many studies on the power of the subconscious mind to work out problems while we sleep or focus on other things. I've even heard psychologists say that the best way to find your lost car keys is to do something else until your subconscious calls up the memory of where you put them. When I learned about programming my goals into my subconscious it was a real epiphany for me. If you say over and over again that you are grateful for achieving a goal, your mind comes to accept that it is entirely possible that you did—or can—achieve that goal.

So that's what I did. I used the past tense like it already had happened.

If you are trying to lose weight, for example, set the goal far enough in advance so that you have time to make it there. Then close your eyes and see yourself stepping on the scale and seeing the weight you want. Or visualize people complimenting you and telling you how amazed they are that you lost all that weight. Don't be afraid to use your imagination. Remember, anything is possible if you put your mind to it and believe.

A few of the goals I wrote down as already achieved on set dates included:

- Losing ten pounds

- Writing an amazing song

- Stopping binge drinking

- No more illegal drugs

IN POPS I TRUST

The Cool Springs crowd included some people of strong faith and a little of that was rubbing off on me, I guess, because I began saying and writing things like, "I achieved all of these goals with God's help." Well, I didn't use the G-word exactly, because I called my vision of God *Pops*. So I'd say that my goals were achieved "with Pop's help."

I call him Pops because he is my true father; my creator. And we've had a special relationship. Whenever I felt lost or needed help or guidance, I could count on Pops. I believe in a higher power, I just decided not to label him like everyone else. Sometimes it's just good to have something to believe in. I've had many private conversations with Pops. You could almost say he's my best therapist. Whenever I've asked for forgiveness, I've gotten it. Whenever I've asked for help, I've had my prayers answered. Now I know that life isn't always fair and we should all be prepared, but for the time being don't be afraid to have something to attach to.

I CALL HIM POPS BECAUSE HE IS MY TRUE FATHER; MY CREATOR.

I wrote my goals on the white board in my Cool Springs home office in October. I also put together a timeline to help me make real progress and even to achieve some of my goals by my birthday in January. One of the goals I had to accomplish by that day was losing ten pounds. As you know, I had wanted to lose about five times that much eventually, but I was working on it under the *eating an elephant one bite at a time* theory.

Complicating this process was the fact that I wasn't able to sit tight in Cool Springs for long stretches. I had to leave my private rehab center to do concerts and promotional events in the U.S. and Europe. I returned whenever I could during breaks and holidays, grabbing a week or two here and there. It was difficult to work on goals on the road, but once I was back in my Tennessee retreat, I refocused and hit it hard.

The funny thing is that once I had my goals in my head and worked on them every spare minute, time just raced by. One day, I returned to the house after being on tour and I realized that a year had gone by since I'd put up the white board and written down my goals—and I'd accomplished every one of them!

I am now perfect and I intend to rest on my laurels the remainder of my life. *I wish!* The truth is, I still have a long way to go, but the funny thing is that doesn't bother me, worry me, or frustrate me at all. I look forward to what lies ahead, the good and the bad. I've come to see challenges as opportunities to test myself and to grow. A big part of it is that once I learned how to set goals and create a plan to go after them, I never again felt lost or out of control. I know that as long as there is another day, there is another way.

I STILL SET NEW GOALS
FOR MYSELF ON A DAILY BASIS.

I still set new goals for myself on a daily basis. I'm always reaching for new achievements. I am constantly challenging myself to be better and to expect victory rather than defeat. Overall, my goal here is to inspire you to keep reaching for greater things, knowing that you deserve the best as long as you are willing to do and be your best.

If you are having difficulty doing that in your current environment because of distractions, temptations, friends who don't share your values, or bad relationships, I suggest that you find your own safe, quiet space to retreat to. If it can't be a cabin in the woods or a place by the beach as we all fantasize about having, then at least find a corner of your room, attic, basement or garage that you set aside for this particular purpose. Be sure to have a goal-setting notebook and a visualization board with you. Or if you are like me and you need to compartmentalize aspects of your life, set aside boxes for each area you want to sort through and improve, just as I used each room in my house to do that. Make your space comfortable and bright. Make it your sanctuary—the haven in your world where you can get away, clear out the clutter and the negativity, set new goals, and create a plan for a better life. I know that you can do it.

PERSONAL NOTES

CHAPTER SEVEN

THE HOUSE OF CARTERS COLLAPSES

I GREW UP always thinking of myself as our family's fixer. I was the eldest child and, as I discussed earlier, my parents often left me in charge of my little brother and sisters while they were working. I felt responsible for them so I became the problem solver for the younger kids, and since our mom and dad argued constantly, I tried to serve, without much success, as their mediator too.

The little kids huddled with me for comfort when our parents fought and talked about divorcing. I was always trying to patch things up, make everyone happy and restore peace. I've already confided that one of the motivations for my early music career was the fact that my performances brought us all together as a family. What I recognize now is that this way of thinking also perpetuated my role as the fixer. My parents and brother and sisters all came to my plays and concerts and, for a while, we felt like what I imagined a normal working class family feels like.

I craved those rare moments of bonding as I was growing up, and even as an adult I found myself trying to make peace, set my siblings straight, or do things that might bring us closer. When big earnings started to flow in from my Backstreet Boy performances, I became both fixer and financier for my family, including my parents, but I quickly saw that I was just subsidizing bad behavior and creating more conflict.

The fact is that we never were anywhere close to being a loving, close-knit family because of all the drinking and fighting and lack of nurturing in our home. Still, fixing my family, collectively and individually, has been one of my overriding missions in life. It's become part of my nature to think about my siblings' well-being even though I should never have had that responsibility heaped on me at such a young age in the first place.

And just because I took on the role of surrogate parent to my brother and sisters doesn't necessarily mean they've always welcomed my efforts in that regard. All too often they've called me a control freak.

My problem was not that I wanted to be in control; I just tried to control the wrong things. It's a mistake many people make, especially if they've felt for a long time that they didn't have rein over *any* aspect of their lives. It seems like kids from broken families often grow up to be control-freak adults who feel compelled to maintain order and micro-manage every situation. I was one of those people until I learned that my efforts to direct other people's actions and lives were misguided. I should have been working on my own actions and life choices instead.

...I JUST
TRIED TO CONTROL
THE WRONG THINGS.

Many of the things that happen to us are simply not within our control. Whether it's a hurricane, a flu virus, or an economic recession, life throws unexpected things at us all the time. We can't control these events, nor can we control most people around us, but we *can* control how we respond to them. The key is to govern what happens on the inside so that you can deal with what happens on the outside.

Obviously, this is not an original concept I came up with on my own. Many therapists, psychologists and spiritual leaders offer advice similar to that of an early self-help guru, Buddha, who wrote: "To enjoy good health, to bring true happiness to one's family, to bring peace to all, one must first discipline and control one's own mind. If a man can control his mind, he can find the way to Enlightenment, and all wisdom and virtue will naturally come to him."

It's such good advice, I wish I'd taken it earlier in life. I'm sure my brother and sisters wished that I had, too. They've never been very receptive to my attempts to control their behavior or to help them. My most public effort to do so was when I brought us all together to appear on *House of Carters*, a 2006 reality show that mercifully lasted for only eight episodes. It originally aired on the E! cable network and on Much Music in Canada.

I WANTED TO RIGHT THE WRONGS, MEND WHAT NEEDED TO BE MENDED, AND HEAL ALL THE WOUNDS OF OUR PASTS.

I'd seen what reality shows had done for Nick Lachey and Jessica Simpson, and then Ozzy Osbourne and his family. I thought this show could be a great vehicle for my brother and sisters as well. I had hoped it would give them wider exposure and help further their careers. We grew up with television as such a big part of our lives that doing a reality show seemed natural. I really didn't anticipate that having billboards with our pictures on them all over Los Angeles would lead to such bad things, or that the attention and celebrity status might spur my brother and sisters to engage in even more self-destructive behaviors. I'd hoped that seeing themselves on television might actually make them want to change for the better.

Going into the show, the plan seemed solid—a win-win for the whole family. None of us mind being in the spotlight, so that wasn't a problem. Aaron and I had our share of media attention already, but our sisters had often wished for their own experiences in the celebrity world. This seemed like a perfect way to make that happen for them. Also, money was an issue for the girls and the show offered them a chance to collect paychecks.

I guess I was delusional for thinking that it might be a fun and profitable way to reunite us, share the limelight and support my siblings. I was simply trying to recreate something—a loving family environment—that I now realize had never really existed for us, except during the briefest of moments in our lives. I wanted to right the wrongs, mend what needed to be mended, and heal all the wounds of our pasts.

Instead of healing old wounds and strengthening bonds, however, the *House of Carters* laid bare all of our family dysfunctions and, I'm sorry to say, only made them worse. I had my own issues at the time, which didn't help my credibility with my brother and sisters. It was a classic case of the blind leading the blind.

What I've learned in more recent years is that my taking on the role of a parent is unfair to my siblings and to me. I was expected to assume more responsibility as an eight-, nine- and ten-year-old than any parent has a right to ask of a child. I was forced out of the big-brother role and into the parental role so early in life that I felt conflicted about it. I wanted to be one of the kids, not one of the parents.

IT WAS A CLASSIC CASE OF THE
BLIND LEADING
THE BLIND.

When I recall my childhood, the happiest times by far were those when I felt free to just be BJ, Leslie, Aaron and Angel's brother, playing video games with them, watching our favorite TV shows, or just goofing around outdoors in the warm Florida sun. The inner conflict I experienced over being handed responsibility for my brother and sisters when I was just a kid myself has been the source of so much of my outer conflict with them over the years.

There's a Bible saying that totally applies to this situation: "Physician, heal thyself!" I know I should have taken that advice at the time, but I didn't. Not entirely. To some degree, I had hoped the show would help refocus me, but *House of Carters* was really my ambitious attempt to bring the warring kids in my family together again as adults. I wanted to help them get their lives on track, even though my own was heading off the rails.

Our parents had divorced. Kevin Richardson had just left Backstreet Boys. I'd been arrested for DUI, my binge drinking and drug abuse were out of control, and I had bounced from one meaningless relationship to the next. It was as if I was a Mr. Fix-it with an empty tool belt.

My siblings and I hadn't lived together in ten years. I was worried that we were growing farther and farther apart, and some of the younger kids seemed a little lost. Aaron, 19, and our sisters Bobbie Jean (BJ), 24, Leslie, 20, and Angel, 19, were struggling to find direction in their lives. My brother, in particular, was associating with some really negative people. We all go through the *bad friend* stage and he was definitely at that juncture in his life.

I was concerned about him because when I was around Aaron's age, I had people who I thought were friends take advantage of me and bring out the worst in me. When you are a celebrity and you aren't careful about who you hang with, the predators move in. They can be very cunning. One person, in particular, crossed a line. We traveled together and even lived together for a while. He knew I didn't like to be alone so he was always available, always ready to roll, to party or to do anything I wanted to do. Then I realized that he'd stolen something of value from me. He admitted that he'd taken it; I'll say that much for him. But even though he came clean, I couldn't trust him anymore.

WHEN YOU ARE A CELEBRITY AND YOU AREN'T CAREFUL ABOUT WHO YOU HANG WITH, THE PREDATORS MOVE IN.

I tried to tell Aaron that there were people like that hanging around him, just looking for whatever they could get from him. Once again, though, Aaron went on the defensive and pointed out that I had big entourages comprised of all kinds of people when I was his age, too.

My efforts to help us all heal together quickly hit a wall because I wasn't in a very good position to doctor anyone else. Time after time I'd come home and there would be strangers in the house and a party under way. When I tried to play the parent and clear everyone out, I got no respect. My family saw me as a control monger, who went out and partied but didn't want them to do the same.

Back then, I just got angry at them for reacting that way because I genuinely thought I was being loving and nurturing. I see now that I was sabotaging my own plan because I wasn't walking the walk. I wanted my brother and sisters' respect, but I was demanding it, instead of earning it. I was still screwing up by not being in complete control of myself and they saw that I hadn't taken the responsibility to lead by example.

It's true that our parents weren't the greatest role models when it came to personal responsibility and nurturing, but I had to get over that. I couldn't keep blaming them. Many people grow up in dysfunctional families and broken homes but still manage to break the pattern and become good mothers and fathers and responsible people. I hadn't yet found the key to breaking that pattern.

LOOKING IN THE MIRROR

In the AA meetings I'd been attending before I came up with the idea of the show, I'd learned to be self-aware and to think more about the consequences of my actions. Those sessions prompted me to look in a mirror and assess what I saw. Unfortunately, the image wasn't pretty. All of the inner troubles and health problems brewing inside of me were manifesting on the outside as well. I could definitely tell I was on the wrong path.

The problem was that I really hadn't figured out at that point how to get back on the right path. But I wanted my brother and sisters to look in the mirror too. Creating a reality show was my way of holding a mirror up to our family, and to each of them as individuals so they'd come to the same realization I'd come to—that something had to change, that we weren't the people or the family we wanted to be.

Thanks to the success of BSB, I had the financial resources and the connections to make a reality show happen. As you know by now though, putting the show together was a lot easier than bringing my family together. My intentions were pure, but I didn't have the credibility or the tools to accomplish what I had set out to do; my brother and sisters quickly let me know that they didn't look up to me the way they once had.

THE FAMILY PLAN

Before the end of the first season, it was evident that my plan had backfired in a big way. So many things went wrong, it's hard to know where to begin telling that sad story. I've since learned that one of the keys to healing your relationships is to focus on what you have in common and on your shared goals, rather than getting stuck on old arguments, hurts and anger. We clearly didn't use that key. Instead, we immediately unlocked the closet where all of the bad stuff from our past was kept.

If you saw more than five minutes of *House of Carters*, first let me say, "I'm sorry." Secondly, let me explain that screaming for my family is like casual conversation for most other families. As I've noted before, our childhood home was almost always in a state of chaos. Between my parents' incessant bickering and the occasional gun firing, there was always a cacophony of noise.

Anyone tuning in to the show saw that my siblings and I picked up that same habit of yelling. We all became combative. We are all hypersensitive about being respected and listened to because we are all very insecure people. We learned to holler and scream just to be heard, just to get our parents to pay attention to us. When they told us to shut up, we accepted it because at least they were acknowledging us.

I NOW PAUSE AND THINK BEFORE I LASH OUT.

Yelling and screaming isn't healthy. It isn't enjoyable. And it isn't very effective as a long-term communications strategy. But it was all we had and it worked better than going to our rooms and crying for hours. Thanks to my reading and my therapists, I now know much healthier, more enjoyable, and more effective ways to communicate in my relationships. I've also learned to recognize the triggers that set off my insecurities and anger so that I don't go into the biological *fight or flight* response.

I now pause and think before I lash out. I take a breath, weigh my responses and choose how I will act rather than letting my emotions dictate my actions. My therapists taught me about neuron bundles in our brains called the amygdala that regulate emotions and how we respond to things that scare us or make us angry. When we feel threatened by something or someone, the amygdala acts like a smoke detector. It senses danger and sets off alarms in another part of the brain that decides how to handle the perceived threat.

Often, people who've been in stressful situations for long periods of time tend to develop very sensitive alarms. As a result, they are hypersensitive. They easily feel threatened or fearful and act without giving their brain time to process and assess the threat. The result is that they frequently over-react, lash out, scream and fight with those around them.

I've learned ways to recognize when my anger or fear is being triggered and to stop and think so I can respond more logically instead of just emotionally. There are ways to mentally turn down the heat generated by your emotions so that you can stay calm and in control of your actions. I'm not saying that I have complete control all the time, but I'm getting better with practice. Unfortunately, I didn't learn these methods before *House of Carters* began taping. We verbally sparred. We screamed at each other. We argued and cried.

And those were the good times.

NOT READY FOR PRIME TIME

Worst of all was a session with a family psychologist I'd brought in to work with us. Again, I was playing Mr. Fix-it, but all that session did was open old wounds. I'd been trying to explain to my brother and sisters that I wanted them to respect each other and to think of me as their brother *the human being*, not as their brother *the celebrity*. I wanted to break down the barriers between us so we could all communicate better. But they felt they knew what they were doing and that I didn't. Every time I'd offer an opinion, they'd either ignore me or point out that I wasn't exactly a great role model.

I felt as if I had no other option but to call in the cavalry. I'm a strong advocate of therapy, so that's when I decided to invite a family psychologist to the set. If it worked for me, surely it would work for my family. But it didn't. We only met with her that once and a therapist needs to spend a lot more time than that to make a difference in someone's life.

When I first spoke with the family psychologist, I told her that I didn't want this show to be a disaster, but it turned out to be a major train wreck anyway. Everyone rolled out horror stories. For instance, Leslie recounted how Mom once tricked her by telling her she was sending her to a summer camp to ride horses, when she was actually sending her to a *fat camp*. Leslie said Mom had hoped to make money from Leslie's singing career, but her weight had become an issue with the record company. That was not the only ugly story shared that day. It was grueling for everyone to rehash those kinds of distressing memories.

While I was accustomed to being on camera and on billboards that make you feel larger than life, the notoriety that came with being on the show lulled my brother and sisters into a false sense of security. They didn't understand that what they said and did on television would never go away, that it would be broadcast all over the world. So, overall, I think the show did much more harm than good. I think it damaged my brother and sisters because they began to think of themselves as stars even though the show wasn't a big hit.

I FELT AS IF I HAD
NO OTHER OPTION
BUT TO CALL IN THE CAVALRY.

The television critics were merciless, though I could hardly blame them. One wrote in *The New York Daily News*, "The only reason for the new reality show 'House of Carters' to exist is to make us all feel better about our own lives. The show, which follows the Carter kids, led by former Backstreet Boy Nick Carter, is nothing but an hour of a severely dysfunctional group of people wallowing in their misfortune. There's not a moment of hope, cheer or any other reason to keep watching."

And not only were the reviews scathing, the ratings for the show weren't great either. I can't even say that the embarrassment was lessened by the limited television viewing audience because sadly, the show still lives on thanks to YouTube and other Internet sources. And, of course, there was the *Saturday Night Live* parody that brought added attention to our family drama. The segment featured Andy Samberg as my brother Aaron, and Jason Sudeikis as me. Mostly they just screamed at each other, hugged each other, and then set back to screaming again.

It wasn't funny, but it was painfully accurate.

MADHOUSE OF CARTERS

For the show, E! rented this huge stone mansion with spectacular views of the Hollywood Hills. In our short time there, we turned a dream house into a madhouse. This beautiful place became party central. Every time I came home from the studio or a concert, it was packed with people. Day and night. Instead of empowering my brother and sister, I was enabling them.

My frustration boiled over into fury. I ranted and raved and came across as a demented dictator most of the time.

IT WASN'T FUNNY, BUT IT WAS PAINFULLY ACCURATE.

On a positive note, there were some unexpected benefits, or at least, enlightenments that came out of the whole experience. I learned a lot about myself just by watching my brother and sisters. Even though I'd spent my first eleven years with them, I was not around all that much once I hit my teenage years. Viewing the reality show and observing their behavior, I realized that we shared many of the same character flaws. We are all very defensive. We all very much want to be loved and appreciated even though we quickly put up walls when we feel threatened, criticized or rejected in any way.

The Carter kids have trust issues. To avoid potential pain, our tendency is to pull back or rebuff the other person first. Staying in control is important to us all, because as kids we felt we had no control over our lives. Our mom and dad were so immature and lacking in parenting skills that we never felt secure, even about where we would live or who would provide for us.

People who put up walls may seem cold or unfriendly to others, but the truth is they often isolate themselves because they feel scared and vulnerable. If you avoid or sabotage relationships for that reason, you should know that you are not responsible for all the things that happened to you. You can't change what you can't control—any more than I could change my brother and sisters by doing that reality show. But you *can* change yourself by controlling how you respond to people and events in your life. You can change your programming. You can learn to react thoughtfully rather than emotionally.

One of the big benefits of this more thoughtful approach is that you won't be as likely to say hurtful things to people you care about. I've had a tendency to say cutting things, especially with my brother and sisters, because I didn't stop to think of the lasting impact those words would have. There is plenty of evidence of this on display in *House of Carters*.

There I was, hoping to mend relationships through the show but instead, every time someone didn't respond the way I wanted them to, I'd say something mean that only made things worse. I can't tell you how many times I've wished that I could take back words I let loose in anger or frustration. So often, I've tried to apologize and just move on, but the damage had been done. You can't lash out at someone and then expect that person to forget what was said. Very few people are capable of forgiving or forgetting so quickly. And when your words hurt them time and time again, you can't blame people for either pushing you away or striking back.

YOU ABSOLUTELY CANNOT MAKE THEM CHANGE.

My attempts to change my brother and sisters didn't work because I hadn't changed myself at that point. How could I expect them to follow my advice when I wasn't following it? After Aaron and I battled it out one day, I realized again that people don't change until they want to change. You absolutely cannot make them change. As the family fixer, that was a hard thing for me to accept, but the *House of Carters* brought the lesson home. Since then, my life has offered proof that dramatic changes can occur, but those changes have to start within you. You can't change another person from the outside in. They have to begin their own process from the inside out.

I showed up to *House of Carters* in full control-freak mode. My brother and sisters rebelled against that, as I should have known they would. They helped me understand that I could not fix them; I could only fix myself. Through that experience and through therapy, I have come to understand that real control begins when you accept that you have no control over anything or anyone but yourself. When you accept that, everything changes. If you don't accept that, nothing will change.

OWNING IT

Thankfully, my life and my relationships have dramatically improved since then because I gave up trying to control others and took responsibility for controlling myself. It's a big change for me and I can't say that I've mastered either part of the equation yet, but I've made progress and I continue to work on it.

I've actually been able to patch things up with Aaron recently and that feels great. Our reconciliation never would have happened if I'd kept trying to change him instead of myself. I just keep repeating the phrase, "Begin from the inside out." Change who you are and people will respond. Heal thyself.

I have admitted my mistakes to my brother and sisters, but even better, I've stopped repeating those mistakes. You can only ask for their forgiveness so many times. Sooner or later, you have to stop hurting them if you expect them to welcome your company. I had to look within and truly acknowledge that I was poisoning our relationships by constantly trying to play the big brother and default parent.

They didn't need me to be the boss. They needed me to be their brother. They didn't need orders or commands. They needed understanding, compassion and empathy. I found that instead of trying to push, shove and force them down the path I wanted them to go, the best thing I could do was walk that path and shine a light for them to follow.

My need to control them was mostly about protecting myself. I was asking them to trust me even though I lacked confidence in myself. That never works. I had to get my own house in order before I could effectively be a leader in the *House of Carters*.

Yes, my insecurities were deeply rooted in my upbringing—the pandemonium I was raised in, and the never-ending fear that my siblings and I would be split up if the divorce my parents threatened actually came to pass. Yet, I had so many experiences that should have made me very confident. I'd begun supporting myself when most kids my age were still in junior high. I'd traveled the world and appeared on stage before millions of people. I'd worked hard to develop my talents and our group had reached the pinnacle of success. We had fans around the world. Why didn't I feel better about myself?

CHANGE WHO YOU ARE AND PEOPLE WILL RESPOND.

I'm sure you have fine points too, yet you may have asked yourself the same question. If you haven't, you probably should. Why do we so often choose to focus on what is lacking in our lives instead of what is there in abundance? Again, it comes down to the power of choice. In the same way that it is better to focus on changing those things within our control rather than wrestling with what is not, you and I have the choice and the power to concentrate on what is good and present in our lives rather than on what is bad or lacking.

SELECTIVE TUNING

With the help of therapy and reading, I've learned to tune out that little cartoon devil that perches on my shoulder whispering negative things in my ears. Instead, I tune into the cartoon angel on the other shoulder who says, *Look what you've accomplished! You've built a great life through your hard work and talents. Feel good about that!*

After the whole *House of Carters* fiasco, I had to make the conscious choice to focus on the only thing that was truly within my control—my own actions and decisions—and hope that my example inspires the ones I love. Part of my personal 'Fix Nick' program is to plug into the positive aspects of my life and future. I invite you to do the same.

I've messed up. I've had to learn many lessons the hard way. But the fact is that now I'm doing better than I ever thought I would. My level of self-understanding is much greater than it's ever been. I think more before I act. I don't let life just sweep me up like a giant wave. I set goals to determine my course and while I don't achieve all those goals, at least I'm taking responsibility for my own failures and successes.

Best of all, I feel I've evolved from the lifestyles of my mother and father. I'm not afraid to admit that the thought of being a parent one day is more than a little scary for me because I didn't have the greatest role models. But I can't control the way I was parented. I can, however, control my own development as a human being. I've come a long way, but I'm not yet fully satisfied. I want to be a loving, nurturing husband and father who encourages his children to seek knowledge and to love themselves.

BUT THE FACT IS THAT NOW I'M DOING BETTER THAN I EVER THOUGHT I WOULD.

You can't stop negative thoughts from coming into your head. But you can control how much attention you give them and how you respond to them. You can choose to ignore any thoughts that bring you down or get in the way of your efforts to be the best you can be. For me, that means getting over what is past—the lack of nurturing and stability in my childhood. I'm sure you have your own baggage, maybe your own hurts, family dysfunctions and failures. We all have things that happened to us, but they don't have to stay with us and weigh us down for the rest of our lives. We can focus instead on moving ahead based on what is good and what makes us better.

Again, it's an inside-out process. When you refuse to live in a negative frame of mind, you project a positive personality and that, in turn, brings more positive things your way in the form of uplifting people, exciting opportunities, and good karma.

Reality check: Bad things will still happen. You can be the most positive person in the world and life will still sucker punch you from time to time. It's okay to feel blind-sided or sad when that happens. It's natural to mourn the loss of a loved one, or to feel down when you experience failures or disappointments. But just remember, this, too, shall pass. Better days will come if you hang in there, stay positive, and focus on being and doing your best.

I remind myself often now that I need to be as good and caring a friend to myself as I am to the other people I love. You wouldn't tell a friend who is struggling that he is not worthy of success. You wouldn't constantly point out what is lacking or bad about her life. Instead, you build up your friends and encourage them by focusing on their talents and strengths. Why wouldn't we do the same for ourselves?

One of the big benefits of being a friend to yourself is that it opens you up to being a friend to those around you. I've learned that when I am more of a friend to myself, I also get along much better with my brother and sisters. I focus on the positive things in their lives instead of the negatives, and I encourage them instead of trying to direct them.

My siblings and I share many of the same dysfunctional behavioral patterns, but we also share many good traits, and many good experiences too. Aaron and I have recently found that when we meet on that common ground, our bonds grow stronger. We feel better about ourselves and about each other when we talk about gratifying, mutual interests, like our music.

Rather than trying to fix what I perceive to be wrong with my younger brother, I'm now trying to focus on listening to him and understanding where he is coming from. The fact is that we are very much alike on many levels, so we get each other. Because I wasn't around a lot in his teenage years—and because I haven't been the greatest role model—he's made many of the same mistakes he's watched me publicly make. Of course, Aaron is another reason I've written this book. It's up to him to avoid some of the pitfalls that I plunged into headfirst, but perhaps the example of how I pulled myself up from those depths can be of some use to him on his own personal journey. The best thing about healing my relationship with Aaron and other family members is that having them back in my life makes me want to be a better person. I want to be there for them. I want them to be proud to share the same last name with me—and that is something I think I can control.

REALITY CHECK: BAD THINGS WILL STILL HAPPEN.

PERSONAL NOTES

CHAPTER EIGHT

HEART SICK

I'M NOT SURE if it was in Moscow or St. Petersburg, but somewhere in Russia during our *Unbreakable* Tour in 2008, I decided I was unbreakable too. I abused my body with booze and drugs like I was indestructible, a human Humvee.

Surprised? I wasn't.

The way I partied on that tour was just crazy, especially since there'd been warning signs that my parts were already out of alignment. I'd been feeling crappy for most of the four months preceding the tour. We'd already done something like forty shows and I was dragging.

I'm a bit of a hypochondriac anyway, but I had plenty of reasons to think something was wrong. I'd hit 224 pounds and was so out of shape that I could hardly catch my breath when we were performing. Then there were the pains in my chest. I'd wake up at night convinced I was having a heart attack, but I'd talk myself down, thinking it was just my hypochondria kicking in.

Did that stop me from binge drinking? No, not Nick Carter. Sad to say, I'd gone back on the bottle just six or seven months after my self-rehab at the Cool Springs house in 2006.

You may remember that I bought the place as a getaway from the Hollywood-party crowd while we were recording part of the *Unbreakable* album.

This was after I'd walked out of Promises, the Malibu rehab center used by many burned out celebrities suffering from the same issues I had. I decided that it would be better to conduct a D-I-Y rehab than to lock myself in with the Promises professionals. As we've already established, I was a control freak at the time and I generally don't like using crutches or relying on other people. Kicking booze and drugs on my own would be a confidence builder, or so I thought.

THEN THERE WERE
THE PAINS IN MY CHEST.

I went for it. For six months I lived like a monk (except for the whole abstinence-from-sex thing). Then I dove headfirst off the wagon and just kept rolling farther and farther down into that big black hole. By the time we launched the world tour behind the *Unbreakable* album in February of 2008, my plan for kicking booze and drugs had been wiped off the whiteboard I'd used successfully back in my Tennessee home.

I did cut back on drugs and pills, though not completely. Mostly, I drank on the tour bus and off it too. I've always had trouble sleeping on the road. Drinking myself into a stupor wasn't the best way to get a good night's rest, but it was my favorite home remedy.

Heavy drinking usually depresses me and makes me paranoid, so you might say I kept pouring gasoline on the fire. In a feat of magical thinking, I used the chest pains as an excuse to get wasted every night. My totally illogical thought process was: *I'm already dying so I'm going to keep drinking and partying.* Apparently, I had decided to go down as a *Nick flambé*, soaked in alcohol and burned out.

MOSTLY, I DRANK ON THE
TOUR BUS AND OFF IT TOO.

That's not a very safe approach anywhere, but it is particularly dangerous in Russia where the locals guzzle huge shots of vodka for breakfast, lunch and dinner. Seriously, I looked it up: Russians drink nearly twice as much as Americans, consuming on average about four gallons of pure alcohol per person annually. There are more than ten million Russians between the ages of 10-14 who drink booze, and about half a million of their people die each year from alcohol-related accidents, crimes or illnesses.

So, while on tour I figured: *When in Russia, drink as the Russians do.* I downed rivers of vodka, but it was the Sambuca that kicked my butt. I was out one night and some locals in a bar were having a last-man-standing contest to see who could down the most shots of the licorice-tasting stuff before passing out. I probably took about 20 shots of Sambuca for the American team. Unfortunately, I missed the medal ceremony. To this day I have no idea how I got back to my hotel.

When I woke up the first thought that hit me was, *Oh my God, I'm dying.* My heart was doing a dance routine in my chest. My lungs felt like someone was stomping the air out of them. My gut was swollen. I didn't have the strength to get out of bed. When I tried, my head started spinning.

I DOWNED RIVERS OF VODKA, BUT IT WAS THE SAMBUCA THAT KICKED MY BUTT.

We were supposed to head to South Africa for four shows after Russia, but Howie Dorough's father, who had been battling lung and brain cancer, took a turn for the worse and was dying. Howie went home to be with him, so we canceled the South Africa shows, which gave us all of June and most of July off before we were scheduled to resume the tour in Canada and the U.S.

In the interim, I grieved for Howie and his family, which led to more boozing. Finding reasons to drink was one of my major skills. I hadn't reached the point where I was getting up in the morning and chugging vodka, but I was headed in that direction. The question that kept running through my mind was whether I'd drink myself to death or die from whatever other illness was making me feel as if an alien predator was feasting on my internal organs.

I headed for Florida during the unscheduled break and went to my doctor for a complete checkup. I ended up in the office of Dr. Richard Polakoff, a Ft. Lauderdale cardiologist, who put me through two days of tests.

I ran on a treadmill with wires taped to me like the *Bionic Man*. By the end of the second day, I was freaked out. Dr. Polakoff wouldn't say much. He kept telling me that no matter what the results were, I needed to change my lifestyle by drinking less, staying off drugs, losing weight, exercising and eating healthier foods. I was told I'd have the results by the next morning.

So, that night, I did my usual sensible thing: I partied like it was my last night on earth. I hit the bars and clubs around Ft. Lauderdale and Miami and went freaking nuts. I drank like I was trying to drown the demons inside my body. Then I did enough blow to make up for the six months I'd stayed clean.

I DRANK LIKE I WAS TRYING TO DROWN THE DEMONS INSIDE MY BODY.

Yeah, that didn't help much.

At least when I went back to Dr. Polakoff's office to get my results, he couldn't say that I looked good for a sick guy. I'm sure I looked like a dead man walking because that's how I felt. Still, I hadn't killed myself.

"Nick, you have a condition known as cardiomyopathy. It's the result of a buildup of toxins in your heart, which weaken it so that it has difficulty pumping blood," he said.

Thinking the worst, I assumed this was a death sentence, but the doctor said mine was not a full-blown case—yet. He told me if I didn't make serious and immediate changes in my lifestyle, the toxins would eventually kill me. He explained that it has killed a lot of young guys who partied like me, including the singer Andy Gibb and the actor Chris Penn. "We don't want you to end up like them," said Dr. Polakoff.

"I don't want to end up like them either," I told him.

I was so relieved that it wasn't cancer or something worse that I didn't take the doctor's warning seriously. I headed for South Beach instead.

You are probably thinking: *Nick has a death wish.*

Maybe I did. Bad news. Good news. It didn't matter. Booze and drugs were my answer to every situation and every occasion. South Beach was the perfect place for death-wish fulfillment. I drank, did drugs, and partied until I was paralyzed and passed out.

I woke up in a hotel room with my head pounding so hard I couldn't focus my eyes. The room was all white; so white, I wondered if I was in a casket, dead and buried six feet under.

If I'm not dead, I should be and if I don't stop this, I will be soon.

My heart was pounding so loud I thought someone was at the door. I decided my body was trying to get my attention one last time. I stayed in bed, flat on my back, trying to slow the battering inside my chest with deep breaths. My doctor's warnings played out in my head.

Andy Gibb died of cardiomyopathy at 30.

I was 29.

Every time I binged on alcohol and drugs, it weakened my heart. The doctor said if I kept it up, my energy level would keep dropping until one day my heart would just stop. They call it *sudden death disorder*, but I'd been slowly crawling toward death for a long, long time. If I had died of this, my tombstone should have said, "He wasn't so *unbreakable* after all."

I hadn't listened to the warnings of Kevin Richardson, Brian Littrell, or any of the people closest to me. The DUI hadn't done it. The horrible Night of the Zombies didn't do it either. I'd stayed mostly clean for six months but then I'd fallen farther and deeper than ever before.

...I WONDERED IF I WAS IN A CASKET, DEAD AND BURIED SIX FEET UNDER.

Now I was poisoning my own heart. The binge drinking and drugs were pumping toxins into it—and so was all of the lingering bitterness, resentment, and anger I felt toward my parents.

I needed a massive physical, mental, and emotional detox. I stayed in bed for hours, trying to calm my heart and stop the marching band in my brain. When I finally had the strength, I packed my stuff, checked out of the hotel, got in my car and headed for Cool Springs.

This time, I had no choice. It was change or die.

BREAKABLE

If you've ever thought you were indestructible and that you could binge drink, do drugs, and just keep partying because nothing would bring you down, think again. I was committing suicide and so are you if you continue to follow that crazy lifestyle. There is nothing cool about a death wish. It is just a waste of a life and a stupid, stupid thing to harbor.

IT WAS CHANGE OR DIE.

I was great at justifying my self-destruction, though. For the longest time, it was my parents' fault. I was the victim of their horrible parenting, their bad examples, and their broken marriage. Then, the justification sort of shifted into: *I'm sick and dying, so I might as well drink and do drugs.*

Either way, I was taking my own life.

Guys and girls in their teens and twenties are probably the worst when it comes to abusing their bodies and endangering their health, whether it is with alcohol, drugs, poor eating habits or lack of exercise. Males in general tend to think it's unmanly to have regular checkups and to eat healthy foods.

I was a serial offender in the health department until just the last few years when my toxic heart gave me a cold, harsh reality check. I seriously never thought drinking and doing drugs could infect my heart. Then again, I didn't think much at all about consequences of any kind.

That's yet another mistake I made so you don't have to. Well, maybe not exactly, but I certainly hope you learn from me and consider the devastating effects of drinking and doing drugs. Scientists who study the human brain say that generally young people in their teens and early twenties are lacking in their ability to see the consequences of their actions or to have a long-term perspective because their brains are literally re-wiring themselves during those years. Old connections are cut off and new ones are being formed up until around the age of 25.

So, maybe *that's* my excuse?

Though any rationalization I could possibly dream up doesn't really matter because damage was done. Only time will tell if it was irreparable.

And only time will tell what further toll my excesses may have taken on my body. Remember that I still sweat the fear of Ecstasy's unforeseen effects.

I hope you don't have similar concerns. Even if you do, though, your choices are the same as mine. All we can do now is work to repair the damage that is possible to repair, and keep ourselves as healthy as we can in the hope that our bodies will forgive the abuse and neglect of years past.

Unless you've been through a serious illness or had someone close to you spend weeks in the hospital, you probably haven't thought about what it's like to lose your health. But when you are truly sick or in chronic pain, everything else in your life changes. Your dreams are put on hold. There is no such thing as going out and having fun. You are miserable all the time.

Why would anyone risk that? Most people (men especially, but women too) don't want to face the realities of their health. They tell themselves that bad things can't happen to them. Cemeteries are full of people who thought they'd never get sick and die. The reality is, it happened to them and it can happen to you. I'm not unbreakable or bulletproof and neither are you. So here are a few basic suggestions that I hope you will take to heart.

GET A CHECKUP BEFORE YOU CHECK OUT

See a doctor at least once a year for a checkup. If something doesn't seem right, talk to your doctor about it. Denial can be deadly. I'm sure you've heard someone say of a friend or family member who'd died: "If only he'd gone to a doctor . . ."

Checkups are no fun, but most things that can kill you can be slowed, stopped, or even reversed if detected early enough. A doctor can tell you, just as Dr. Polakoff told me, if you are doing something that is endangering your health. I probably would have died within a few years if I'd kept drinking and doing drugs like I was back then.

I'm not perfect now. I still slip up when it comes to drinking. But I'm alive and great things have happened for me in the last few years. I would have missed them. I'm glad I didn't. Take care of yourself so you'll be present for the great things in your life, too.

GET YOUR DRINKING UNDER CONTROL

Stop binge drinking and drinking until you're drunk. If you can't control it, stop all together. You will need help to do that. Remember there is no shame in asking for help. Alcoholics Anonymous or a trained therapist can save your relationships, your job, and your life by helping you find alternatives to drinking alcohol. They've done it for millions of people. I'm one of them.

You may not think you are worthy of living or being sober. AA can help you with that too. In the meantime, think about all of the other people you are putting in danger when you drive drunk, or go to work intoxicated or hung-over. I didn't want to be that person. Nor did I want to be the person in the newspaper article or obituary that makes readers wonder, "Why didn't he stop drinking and doing drugs before it came to this?"

My generation may be the most drugged of all time. Early in elementary school, I saw kids in my classes taking drugs prescribed to treat hyperactivity, Attention Deficit Disorder, or both. There's no doubt that many kids benefitted from these medicines, which kept them focused and alert, but there were also a lot of kids who abused them. Once it was discovered that these drugs could help you lose weight, study for exams more easily, or just give you a good high, some kids would go to their doctors and fake symptoms in order to get prescriptions, which

MY GENERATION MAY BE THE MOST DRUGGED OF ALL TIME.

they would subsequently misuse themselves or sell to their friends. My generation became all too comfortable with pill popping. But self-medicating is a dangerous trend, especially when kids buy pills from each other. On the street, there is little control over the dosage or even the chemical contents of the pills. A lot of these drugs are safe in controlled and prescribed amounts, but incredibly dangerous when sought from unknown sources and taken too often or in large quantities. In my experience, I've seen many people who have used drugs prescribed for ADD and hyperactivity, who then see taking Ecstasy, prescription painkillers, cocaine and meth as just another step up the ladder.

These people take drugs without giving any thought to the long-term effects, until it's too late. Are you headed for the place where you want to end up? Or are you headed for a panic attack, a heart attack, or something worse?

Smoking cigarettes is another crazy thing we do to ourselves. There is no excuse any more for doing that since we all know it is suicide, plain and simple—especially if you have a family history of lung cancer. There are many programs out there to help you stop smoking. Your doctor can recommend the best for you. Trust me, if I can quit by wearing a t-shirt with a stop-smoking message, you can find a way too. Bottom line: Do you really want to hack, cough, wheeze and slowly suffocate yourself to death?

Smoking isn't the only way we can slowly kill ourselves, of course. The junk we eat can take us down too.

I WAS A JUNK FOOD JUNKIE

My name is Nick and I was a snack-food-aholic. Also, a sugary cereal fanatic, and a potato-chip-crunching-machine. I only dined at the finest of cheap, fast-food restaurants. There is nothing wrong with eating a cheeseburger, pizza or taco now and then as long as you are getting plenty of exercise too. But if you eat greasy fried foods all the time, the fat, sugars and chemicals will take a toll on your body. Now that I am eating healthier, I can tell the difference both physically and emotionally because the chemicals in junk foods can affect your mood too.

One of my big mistakes during my party days was stuffing myself late at night. I've learned that you really shouldn't eat after sundown if you want to stay in shape. That's a hard rule to follow because most adults don't get home from work until much later than that and their families suffer, too, because they wait to eat together. My metabolism slows way down around seven at night so in the old days when I would eat much later than that, I was getting fatter as I slept. Now I try not to take unburned calories to bed with me.

Today, I'm a healthy-diet convert, a reformed fast-food junkie, and erstwhile late-night munchies king. There are a zillion nutritional plans out there, and maybe there is one that will work for you better than the others. The basic rule is just to be very conscious about what you eat and how often you eat.

I exchanged chicken wings, pizza, chips, and fries for egg-white omelets, grilled chicken, and veggies. I don't mind sharing that I also became a master at counting calories. I went online and found the forms and the calorie count for just about everything edible so I could keep track of exactly what I put into my body. For me, that was half the battle. I was shocked to learn that many of the foods I thought were healthy and low-calorie were not. Apples are nutritious but they are not low in calories. One small apple is about 60 calories. A banana is about 75. Then again, a typical cream-filled cake snack is about 250 calories—and I was known for eating two boxes of them in one sitting!

...THE WEIGHT DIDN'T COME OFF EASILY.

I wasn't just a binge drinker. I was a binge eater too. I'd get drunk or high, or just sad, and I'd start popping things in my mouth as fast as I could. I'd eat because I was depressed, and then I'd be even more depressed because I was so overweight and out of shape.

Like most young guys, I hadn't paid much attention to calories. But I learned that you only need about 1,800 to 2,000 calories a day to sustain you if you are a generally healthy person. That's enough to just break even on a daily basis if you don't exercise a lot. To lose weight you have to eat less or exercise more, and sometimes both.

Eating less food doesn't mean cutting down on your meals. I actually began eating every three hours, but my portions were smaller and the menu options were composed of mostly healthy carbs with low sugar content because sugar releases insulin that makes you hungry.

I cut my calories by about 500 per day and exercised for an extra hour or two. I was lucky enough to work with a trainer and a nutritionist to achieve just the right balance to insure that I was burning calories and losing pounds, but there are many fine books and tapes out there that can guide you to do the same. Even with their help, the weight didn't come off easily. For a while it seemed like the scale was stuck. But I kept setting small goals and slowly increasing them. I started out just trying to lose a pound a week. Achieving those attainable goals always gave me a little boost.

If you are like me and tend to eat when stressed, try to be conscious of that impulse. Instead of heading to the refrigerator or the pantry, go to the gym, watch a movie, or at least substitute healthier snacks for the junk food. I lost my belly fat by swapping fast food for healthier fare and by making sure I exercised at least five times a week.

I also visualized myself getting thinner, and I thought every day about how much better I would feel and look when I lost my gut and excess body fat. I'd look in the mirror and imagine myself in a whole new body with a slimmer waist and a thinner face. I'd see it and then I'd believe it was possible, and once it was imprinted on my subconscious, I made smarter food choices, I worked out consistently every day and my body responded in kind.

Soon, people were noticing and saying things, and within six months the excess weight was gone. Now, I know it won't be that simple or easy for most people. I have a body type that lends itself to being thin. I was also fairly young, and my food choices before that had been so awful that any improvement was bound to garner results. But I know some people have thyroid challenges, metabolism problems, and other medical factors to deal with. If you do have any of these issues, your doctor or a nutritionist can help you deal with them. All you have to do is be willing to help yourself. It all begins with you.

A BETTER HIGH

The other half of the equation in losing weight is building muscle. The benefits to working out with weights and doing cardio are incredible, but getting into a regular routine can be a challenge if you weren't an athlete at a young age.

I could spend hours on stage performing and dancing but going into a gym to work out was torture for me. Running on a treadmill, track, or on the street had no appeal whatsoever for me, and I thought only muscle heads lifted weights. Even when I worked out with the fitness trainers we hired to whip the guys in the group into shape for a tour, I dreaded it.

ALL YOU HAVE TO DO
IS BE WILLING TO
HELP YOURSELF.

You may feel the same way about exercise. Nobody can make you turn off the PlayStation and go to the Y to workout. You have to want to do it because there is a payback—something pleasurable, worthwhile or beneficial that outweighs the thrill of the joystick or the comfort of the couch.

"Not dying" was the incentive that finally ignited my enthusiasm for exercise. Radical, right? I also figured out that there are ways to build strength and stamina that aren't mind-numbingly boring. Instead of running on a treadmill or jogging, I play basketball for a couple hours. Even weight training doesn't suck if I do it listening to music or with friends who make it fun. Competition always psychs me up more than just working out by myself.

When it seemed like I couldn't knock off the last twenty pounds or so, weight training made all the difference. You shouldn't worry about how much you can lift. It's more about repetitions and resistance. That's what helps you lower body fat. Sure muscle weighs more than fat, but your body will be toned so you will look and feel much better too.

My trainer friends say that when you replace fat with muscle it also cranks up your metabolism so you burn more fat and calories even when you aren't working out. They told me that for every pound of muscle added through lifting weights, I'd burn off as much as one hundred calories more per day.

If you've never worked out with a trainer before, I recommend that you schedule at least one session just so you can learn the proper techniques and be safe. You want to get the maximum rewards for your work, and there is a danger of hurting yourself if you don't learn how to exercise muscle groups correctly. Most trainers will tell you, for example, that you should work your legs one day, then give them a couple of days to rest before working those big muscles again.

One thing that really surprised me was that lifting weights had a much bigger impact on my attitude and self-confidence than I'd anticipated. I've had friends who were big bodybuilders, and they carried themselves with a lot of self-assurance. Once I began to feel stronger and tighter in my arms, shoulder and chest, I understood where that confidence came from. It's a great feeling.

When I first felt and saw the difference in my body, my attitude changed. There is a high that comes with fitness, and it is addictive to a degree. Your body craves it, and that's a good thing. Weight training and cardio exercise not only helps you look better, they also release those really cool endorphins and neurotransmitters, such as serotonin and dopamine, that are thought to block pain and cause feelings of euphoria. Building muscle also increases testosterone, and when you've been in a boy band as long as I have, you can never get enough of that!

"NOT DYING" WAS THE INCENTIVE THAT FINALLY IGNITED MY ENTHUSIASM FOR EXERCISE.

Don't think of exercise as *working out.* Instead, think of it as replacing an unhealthy "high" with a healthy one. I drank and did drugs because I was stressed, angry or bored—all the usual reasons. But the truth is that getting wasted only creates more problems. The next morning I was still stressed, angry, or bored—and I also felt like ten miles of dirt road had been dumped down my throat.

Going to the gym, running, lifting weights, playing basketball, taking hikes, riding bicycles, and other forms of exercise trigger the body's natural stimulants, giving you a healthy high that actually reduces stress and anger, alleviates boredom, and enhances your immune system, helping you sleep better, recover from injuries quicker, and live longer.

Even better: No dry mouth! No pounding headaches! No destroyed brain cells! What a deal!

A certified professional trainer can help you find the fitness regimen best for you. Your local health club, YMCA/YWCA, or area schools offer programs for every body type and budget. If you prefer to exercise at home, I used Bodybuilding.com to create a workout and to track my progress, and I found it really helped keep me on a schedule.

THERE IS A HIGH THAT COMES WITH FITNESS, AND IT IS ADDICTIVE TO A DEGREE.

Since I've committed to a healthier lifestyle, I've been struck by the insanity of my past behavior. I was a genius at coming up with rationalizations for my binge drinking, drug use, smoking, and junk-food habit. Why was it so easy to make excuses for self-destructive behavior but not easy to exercise and eat right? Why did I think doing Ecstasy was a better reward than listening to my favorite music while working out?

CHANGE FOR THE BETTER

Creating a healthier lifestyle is all about replacing what can weaken or even kill you with activities that extend your life and make it more enjoyable. This can include changing your diet and your activities as well as your attitude, your friends and your environment.

I'm about as stubborn as they come, as you've probably noticed. It took the threat of death before I finally made a real commitment to curbing my drinking and drug use, eating healthier, and getting fit. Therapy also helped change my way of thinking. Hopefully, it won't take as much to get your life on a better path. Having a positive attitude is not a sure cure or the answer to all of life's problems. But it is so much better than a negative, self-defeating, self-pitying attitude.

I've mentioned this before, but it's worth repeating: the only way your life will change for the better is if you begin from the inside out. If you are unhappy and unfulfilled, look inside. Clear out the negative thinking, the old hurts, and resentments and bitterness that have led to bad decisions in the past. Make the choice to make a change in your attitude. Use whatever motivation is available to you, but use it to take positive actions that make you feel better about yourself.

I'M ABOUT AS STUBBORN AS THEY COME.

Getting out of the Hollywood party environment was a major step in the right direction for me. I've stayed away from my old Tampa social circles, too. I mean no disrespect to those friends, but the old ways I engaged in were bad for me. I wasn't strong enough to resist the temptations that came with those people, and the places where we hung out.

Cool Springs is a much healthier environment for me. Bad temptations aren't nearly as prevalent. I don't have to use all sorts of energy just to stay out of trouble. I can relax. My Tennessee friends are more about music and family and spiritual things. They make me want to be a better person. They are the type of friends I need at this point in my life, and probably for the rest of my life, too.

When I committed to making changes in my attitude, my health, my environment and my friendships, I discovered something that I'm pretty sure will happen to you too: totally unexpected good stuff begins to happen on a regular basis. And in a way it makes sense. If you binge drink, do drugs, hang with a partying crowd, and spend most of your time in bars and clubs, trouble is bound to find you. It sure found me. So, it stands to reason that if you take care of your body by not abusing drugs and alcohol, working out, hanging with positive and productive people in places like nice restaurants, health clubs, and at home, good things will find you.

I've been a lucky guy in many, many ways, but I've never had such a great run as I've experienced since I became more devoted to cleaning up my act. I still mess up at times. I'm not saying I'm perfect and that my life is all sunshine and roses. Still, in this next chapter, I'll share with you some of the cool things that have come my way since I've worked on the new, improved, fat-free, and drug-free Nick.

I'VE BEEN A LUCKY GUY IN MANY, MANY WAYS...

PERSONAL NOTES

CHAPTER NINE

THE COMEBACK

I BEGAN THIS book by telling you how great it felt to be on stage during the Central Park concert that kicked off the Backstreet Boys 20th anniversary reunion tour. We were back in more ways than most people realized.

Although BSB never broke up or shut down operations completely, we did take a two-year hiatus from 2002 to 2004. Then in 2006, Kevin Richardson decided to focus on acting and other projects. When he rejoined us in 2012, it was a legitimate comeback and reunion because all of the original members were performing together again.

IN TRUTH, I'D BEEN
THE WEAK LINK IN
THE CHAIN FOR QUITE A WHILE.

At least that's the way most outsiders saw it. However, the members of the group actually have a little different perspective on the situation. We saw the 2012 tour as a reunion in which not one but *two* members of the original group returned. There was Kevin, and then there was me: the real me, or actually, maybe the new, grown-up me.

After Kevin left in 2006, the rest of us continued touring and recording albums. We worked constantly to keep the BSB flame stoked. But

I was sucking all the oxygen from the fire with my burnout behavior. The tabloids had it right: I was the lost boy in the Backstreet Boys.

In truth, I'd been the weak link in the chain for quite a while. There is no real way to prepare for the life of a pop star I suppose, but especially when you have no tools in the toolbox for dealing with the worst temptations and excesses served up by the celebrity life.

BUT I WAS SUCKING ALL THE OXYGEN FROM THE FIRE WITH MY BURNOUT BEHAVIOR.

Can you remember being 12 years old? Did you have your act together at that age? Was the way you saw the world then much different than the way you see it now? Imagine spending most of your teen years without any strong parental presence, and with just about anything you wanted within your reach. That life does not suck at all. I'm not saying that.

Traveling the world. Singing to thousands and thousands of people. Being part of an amazing group of talented guys. Always being treated like someone special. What an incredible, awesome life! I was blessed beyond belief, no doubt about it.

I just wish I'd handled myself better. Being the youngest in the group, I got away with a lot. The eldest, Kevin, who is nine years older than me, treated me like his wayward kid brother. All the guys were protective and patient with me. I loved performing and I worked hard alongside them during the first five years or so. Then, my joy and gratitude gave way to darker feelings.

THEN, MY JOY AND GRATITUDE GAVE WAY TO DARKER FEELINGS.

When I look back at the hours and hours we spent in studios recording, touring around the world, and maintaining our crazy lifestyle, I really don't know how any of us kept our heads on straight. My teen years flew by so fast. I was living the dream, no doubt about it. I was well trained as a singer, dancer and stage performer. I just wasn't very well grounded as a person.

There aren't many teens who have life all figured out. We all need those years to decide who we are, where we fit in, and what sort of people we want to become. The teens who are luckiest are the ones whose parents try to guide them, provide boundaries, rein them in when needed, and of course encourage and support them, too.

For all of the wonderful things that came my way, I didn't have that sort of backup. I don't want to rehash all the stuff I've told you already about my challenges with my parents. The point I want to make here is that we all make mistakes and do stupid stuff, but it is possible to turn your life around. While I'm not all the way there yet, I'm much better than I was. And I'm working on it every day.

YOU CAN RECLAIM YOUR LIFE IF YOU ARE WILLING TO ADMIT YOUR MISTAKES.

So if there is one take-away from this chapter and this book, it is this: it's never over. Not unless you are dead and buried. You *can* get sober. You *can* heal. You can reclaim your life if you are willing to admit your mistakes. You *can* make the necessary corrections, and repair the damage done to your relationships and your reputation.

TOUGH LOVE

My comeback wouldn't have been possible if the other guys in Backstreet hadn't been willing to forgive me. We all had our bad days. We all made mistakes that put strains on our relationship, but I was definitely the problem child for a long stretch. I was just off my rocker for a while.

You already know about the arrest in Tampa, the DUI in California, and my self-administered rehab in Tennessee. Those were the highlights—or the lowlights as the case may be—but there was plenty of other embarrassing crap in between. What I haven't really described before is how my craziness affected Backstreet and my relationship with the guys. Most of it didn't make headlines and none of it was super-terrible, just unnecessary and self-destructive.

179

Sometimes it was expensive, too. In January of 2004, we began recording our *Never Gone* album, the follow-up to our huge *Black and Blue* album. Actually the title *Never Gone* was inaccurate because I was *way* gone during much of the recording of it. One hint that something was missing was the fact that we cranked out the *Black and Blue* album after about three months of studio work, but it took a year to finish *Never Gone*. Even when I was there physically, I wasn't at full strength mentally or emotionally due to all the partying, romantic ups and downs, and family issues in my life.

I was not the only one who missed studio sessions, or showed up late and in less than prime working condition, but I was definitely the worst repeat offender. I wasn't into writing music and recording songs. I was into drinking in bars, partying, doing drugs and generally not caring about my life. This was around the time I broke up with Paris Hilton and I began my serious decline.

It wasn't as though I thought Paris was the love of my life. As I said earlier, we had some good times, but all too often I felt like I'd been abducted by an alien life form and taken to a planet where money is no object and hard work and paying bills are somebody else's problems.

THE CHALLENGE WAS:
I DIDN'T KNOW
WHERE I BELONGED.

Did I get sucked into that life for a while? Yes, guilty as charged. But I quickly realized I didn't belong there. The challenge was: I didn't know where I belonged. That's what set me off in the downward spiral where it seemed I kept piling one mistake on after another.

I was constantly in a fog. I skipped rehearsals or showed up hours after our start time. Finally, when our manager Johnny Wright couldn't get me to straighten up any other way he cracked down: "Nick, if you don't show up or you're late, it's a thousand dollar fine every time."

My slacker response was predictable: "Whatever."

The bad news for the other guys was that Johnny had to enforce it for everyone in the group to make it seem fair, even though I was his primary offender. This was during a time when my financial affairs were just as messed up as the rest of my life. I'd been giving money away, wasting it, making bad investments and generally not paying enough attention.

So, when we finished the album and Johnny handed out the tabs for our fines, I was not exactly prepared to write a check. The total for all of the guys in the group was $80,000. My share was $60,000!

That got my attention. Johnny, who donated the money to a charity we selected, was giving me tough love, trying to shock me out of my negligence and irresponsibility. The message came through loud and clear and stuck with me, too. When word got out around the music business, I was embarrassed.

Johnny's attack on my wallet finally got my attention. His one thousand dollar penalties worked on several levels. Aside from the humiliation, there was the impact on my finances. Every dollar of mine that went toward the fines was another reminder of my increasing irresponsibility and self-sabotaging behavior.

Fortunately, Backstreet has been a very resilient group. We know each other so well. We are loyal to each other. There is a great deal of patience and understanding among the guys, which is a good thing for me.

They never said they wanted to kick me out of the group, though there were many times I deserved it. They just kept hoping I'd figure it out because they knew that was the only way I'd change. We've allowed each other room to grow over the years. We've seen each other through some really hard times.

TALKING IT OUT

At one point, right after my breakup with Paris, I went on a major bender. I skipped rehearsals and stayed out drinking for two consecutive days and nights. I had it in my head that I wanted to quit the group. I was over it and I told that to Johnny and his business partner Ken Crear, who later became my manager.

They came to my house to find out what was going on and I just let loose with all of my frustrations and anger. Most of it had nothing to do with the guys in the group or Johnny or Ken. I knew they were just trying to keep the fires going. It was all about my inability to control my drinking and drug use and my relationships. I felt utterly lost.

Johnny and Ken told me I could quit the group if I wanted to, but they helped me see that it was really my breakup with Paris and other personal issues that were causing my depression. They said that instead of sitting around and wallowing in my misery, I'd be better off focusing on the good things in my life, like my work with BSB. They were right, of course.

When you're down and sinking fast, just changing your focus can make a huge difference. When bad things happen in one aspect of your life, whether it's your relationship, or your job, or an illness, or even the loss of someone you love, the best thing to do is to find a more positive focus for at least part of your day.

Grieving a loss is important, and there is a time and a place for it. But if you feel yourself sliding into depression or despair, then you should take a break now and then. Exercising, reading an upbeat story, watching a funny movie, or having a meal or coffee with someone who makes you laugh can work wonders.

GRIEVING A LOSS IS IMPORTANT, AND THERE IS A TIME AND A PLACE FOR IT.

The sad times are the times to turn to your best friends and those who truly care about you. Listen to their encouraging words and suggestions. They want you to thrive and succeed. After my talk with Johnny and Ken, I realized that the best thing for me would be to get back to the studio and back on stage doing what I loved for the people who appreciated our music. I snapped out of it and I was incredibly grateful for their advice.

Now, it's also true that depression is a serious mental health issue and you may need professional help if things get really dark for you. If focusing on positive things and being around people who care about you doesn't lift your spirits, I encourage you to talk to someone trained to deal with depression, whether it's a therapist, psychologist, psychiatrist, member of the clergy, or a counselor of some kind.

I was lucky that Johnny and Ken let me vent my feelings, and that they leveled with me. They were worried about me personally and professionally. They told me I was on the verge of destroying my friendships and my career. Basically, they conducted an intervention without having some strong-armed guys haul me off to rehab. They had a financial interest in straightening me out, sure, but I knew they cared about me too. Johnny had been with us since BSB came together in Orlando. He'd watched us grow up and he'd worked hard to keep us all on track. He'd also stepped in to manage my brother Aaron, so he knew my family's history. I'm sure Johnny knew more about us than he wanted to in that regard.

LISTEN TO THOSE WHO CARE

Did our talk help? It did. I think just laying everything out there and expressing how you feel can help open the door to healing. When someone reaches out to you, even if they are angry with you and ready to give up on you, don't return their anger. You may have earned it. Take the opportunity to hear them out and to let them hear you out. Try to get to the root of the problem and be aware that the problem could very well be you, not them.

That was my story. I was afraid of burning out. I'd worked as a performer from such a young age. The success we had with Backstreet was incredible, but you do get caught on a treadmill of sorts, trying to keep the success going, afraid to stop or let up. I'm not asking for sympathy or trying to convince you that my life as a pop star was difficult. The only problem with it was the person I'd become. I didn't want to be the guy who wasted his talents and blessings, but for whatever reasons I couldn't stop my slide into the abyss.

This sort of thing happens a lot in the music and entertainment industry. You see people who became stars at a young age get lost. Often it's because they don't have an anchor. They don't have the family support, or the moral or spiritual roots to go back to whenever they need direction. Kevin Richardson and Brian Littrell are very open about how their Christian faith has kept them strong over the years. Seeing how they drew upon their beliefs to handle their own challenges made me ultimately respect and appreciate their strong spiritual backgrounds. I've tried to take bits and pieces of their belief systems and use them in building my own foundation.

There are several younger performers who appear to be handling success well on their own terms. I don't know Justin Bieber, and maybe things will change for him down the road, but my impression is that he is pretty well grounded. I'm glad to see him set a good example. Taylor Swift is another young performer who seems to have it together. Now they may prove me wrong, but from what I've seen they are handling stardom with much more finesse than I ever did at their ages. The tabloids feed off those who don't do so well in the celebrity environment. Too often, I see those who started young either burn out because they exhaust themselves trying to stay in the limelight or because they never felt deserving of it. Of course, those who crash and burn make the headlines while the people who adjust and keep growing or find another path generally do so quietly and with class.

SHARED COMEBACK

The Backstreet Boys held together because the guys were patient with each other and with me. They kicked my butt now and then. They told me they were disappointed with me when I needed to hear it, but they let me find my way back.

THE BACKSTREET BOYS HELD TOGETHER BECAUSE THE GUYS WERE PATIENT WITH EACH OTHER AND WITH ME.

In the bad times, I just wouldn't show up to rehearsals or recording sessions. I wouldn't even call to cancel or to apologize. The guys and our managers lost trust in me and that's a terrible thing. It takes years to rebuild those bonds—years of consistently showing that you are no longer unreliable or that you are no longer that person.

One of my blind spots in the bad years was my failure to see the difference between who I thought I was, and the Nick Carter everyone else knew. I saw myself as a good guy, a caring person, a little mixed up and immature, but someone who would never intentionally hurt another human being. I thought I was that Nick Carter, but in truth, that was just the guy I *wanted* to be.

I had trouble understanding why people didn't trust me because I considered myself trustworthy. There again, I was oblivious to the reality. My actions didn't match up to my self-image. We can't expect others to accept us and trust us just because we have good intentions. We have to deliver.

You can't demand that your friends and family members care about you and offer their help if you only take from the relationship. You have to contribute just as much or more than you take. In fact, if you've been taking and not contributing, then you may have to put in a couple of years of just giving to earn your way back in.

MY ACTIONS DIDN'T MATCH UP TO MY SELF-IMAGE.

Good intentions are a great start, but you are measured and judged by your actions. The word for this is *integrity*. It's about making sure your actions match the image you project. I'm sure you've met charming and persuasive people who win your trust with their words, but then you quickly see their actions don't align with those words. They may claim to have your best interests at heart, but the interests they serve are their own. For too long, I coasted along on my good intentions. I expected my friends and fellow BSB members to be understanding and sympathetic when I fell short, but you can't burn people time after time and expect them to forgive you. They have to protect themselves.

How do you repair a damaged friendship or family relationship? Knowing yourself is important, but understanding how the other person perceives you and feels about you is even more critical. Part of my problem with my brother and sisters was that for a long time, I thought showing my love to them meant giving them what they said they needed. The challenge there is that most of what they came to me for was money or material things. At first, I gave it to them, but then I saw that wasn't really what they needed. They took those things for granted and, in some cases, just wanted more. I had to learn to look past the things they were requesting and instead, try to understand what their emotional needs were, which is a more challenging thing to do.

I've also tended to reach out to them with grand gestures like the reality television show when, in truth, it's the little things you do for people that really build trust and mutual respect. Being there when you say you will be there, doing what you've promised to do, giving of your time and attention; those are the things that build bridges between you and those you care about.

Similarly, I had to build bridges between the guys in the group and myself. I had to find a way to regain their trust. I had to let them know I would follow through on my responsibilities. I lacked good examples of this throughout my life so I had to find my own way and sadly, it took a long time. Too long.

I was a passive member of BSB for longer than I can remember. I didn't want to write songs or take a leadership role. Part of it was my age, being the youngest, and part of it was just not being focused on the right things. It's interesting that my personal comeback and the group's comeback coincided in many ways.

A NEW SONG

One symbol of that mutual revival is a song I wrote in October of 2012 while we were recording our 20th anniversary album. We'd been invited to perform at Disneyland for a Christmas special and there was talk about redoing an old holiday-themed song we'd done. I offered instead to write a new one because I'd always wanted to write a Christmas song. I made my case by noting that we wouldn't be releasing the first single from the new album until next spring, so it might be good to get another song out to give our fans something special before then.

I think Kevin, Brian, Howie and A.J. were a little surprised because I didn't usually pipe up like that when it came to writing for the group. I also suspect they had their doubts that I'd actually come through with something we could put out. Given my checkered past, I couldn't blame them. But I used that as motivation, promising them that I would deliver a song they'd be proud to perform—even in public!

Christmas songs may be lighter than most of our material, but we still had to meet a certain standard. We always want to put out great songs no matter what the genre is. When I told the guys I was going to write them a truly great piece their general reaction was like, *Whatever Nick, we'll need to have a backup song just in case.* They didn't come out and say what they were thinking, but you could tell they were wondering, *Can we really count on you this time?*

I really had to prove myself to them and that was okay. I had to earn their trust again because I'd disappointed them so often in the past. You can't let yourself get angry or bitter in a situation like that. Part of creating a better life is taking responsibility for past mistakes and broken promises.

PART OF CREATING A BETTER LIFE IS TAKING RESPONSIBILITY FOR PAST MISTAKES AND BROKEN PROMISES.

Like the song says, *Oh Lord, it's hard to be humble.* But humility can be very helpful if you are attempting to reclaim lost trust and lost respect. Humility also comes easier if you mix in some gratitude. I was grateful that I still had the opportunity to pitch a song as a member of BSB. The guys had kept me in the group even when I hadn't deserved it or appreciated it, so I was okay with proving myself.

HUMBLE GOALS

Many people have a sense of entitlement. They think everyone owes them their trust and their respect. It's not that way, I'm afraid. You have to earn those things, and if you somehow lose them, you've got to figure out how to fight to get them back. I'd taught people that they couldn't depend on me. I had to accept that and then work on teaching them that I'd changed for the better.

In this case, I taught them by winning them over with my song. I knew I couldn't just throw one on the table and expect them to record it even if it sucked. So I set the bar high. I aimed to write a song we'd be proud to put out as a single or on an album. Yes, I set a goal, which was another sign to the other guys that I was a new and improved Nick Carter. Drunks and slackers don't set goals, other than to drink more and do less. You have to feel good about yourself and your future to set goals. It took me a while to get to a place where I felt comfortable doing that, but I did.

The key is to take small steps—even baby steps at first. I took mine back at the Cool Springs house. I described earlier how I wrote a series of goals on the whiteboard. Initially, most were small goals. My comeback trail was a long-term one. There were some detours and dead ends along the way. I got lost a couple of times. I ran into a few walls and even drove off the road once or twice.

MY COMEBACK TRAIL
WAS A LONG-TERM ONE.

That might happen to you too. I hope it doesn't, but you shouldn't make the mistake of thinking rebuilding and reclaiming your life will be easy or free of failures and disappointments. And don't feel like you have to make your comeback all on your own. It starts with you, no doubt about it, but those who truly care about you will buy in once they see you are serious and committed to being better and doing better.

I asked Howie to work on the song with me. A couple of other guys who were working on the album—songwriter Mika Guillory and producer-songwriter Morgan Taylor Reid—helped too. At first I'm sure they were thinking, *Oh God, what is crazy Nick up to now?* We were supposed to be working on songs for the new album, not some single release. Our studio time was limited. So, I got right to it. I pulled a guitar off the wall and played around until I found three chords I liked. The four of us messed around for fifteen or twenty minutes and the chord patterns and melody emerged and formed into a song. The lyrics flowed once we had the music. Within the hour, we had the song: "It's Christmas Time Again." That's the magic of working with talented people in a studio.

Later in the day, I presented the song to the rest of the guys. We tinkered with it a little more. Once we had it polished, we decided we'd perform it for the first time on November 4th during the taping of Disney Parks Christmas Day Parade at Disneyland. We then sang it for the first time on national television during our November 14th appearance on *The Talk*. The song was so well received, we followed up by performing it again five days later on *Late Night with Jimmy Fallon*. It was amazing to hear Jimmy say backstage, "I loved the song" and that it was one of the reasons he wanted us to perform. My heart was filled with happiness. I had come such a long way. And to receive a compliment from someone that I'm such a huge fan of made my Christmas, no pun intended.

Fans and critics seemed to like the song. Artistdirect.com gave it five out of five stars and called it a "timeless Christmas anthem." The song also hit No. 1 on *Billboard's* Holiday Digital Song chart. Every song is a collaborative effort, but I felt a great deal of pride in the creation of this one. After too many years of letting down my friends and myself, I delivered on a promise. I came up with the idea and, with a little help, I made it happen.

I CAME UP WITH THE IDEA AND, WITH A LITTLE HELP, I MADE IT HAPPEN.

I've been inspired by the success of that song and the great feelings I took away from the experience of conceiving, creating, and performing it. As I write this, we are still working on our new album to be released in 2013. We've recorded about thirty songs so far and I've helped write about 75 percent of them.

Every time I create another song, I feel like I grow as a person and as an artist. It would be great if "It's Christmas Time Again" became a classic. What really mattered at the time though, was that I proved to the other guys in the group, and to myself, that I could be trusted and relied upon. That is so important to me as I look ahead to better days.

The old Nick would never have been so engaged in writing songs and putting an album together. I am so happy to finally be able to do that. We're at a critical stage as a group. After twenty years, we reached the point where we are stepping up to take charge of our brand like never before.

Instead of relying on the label to direct our careers, we're taking charge and showing that we're fully capable of finding our own material and managing our own careers. Now when the label's executives and A&R (artist and repertoire) team come to us with their ideas, we step up and tell them what sound and material we think will work best. I'm enjoying being in the lead with my boys these days.

CHANGE BEGINS WITH YOU

If you want to change your life and become a better person, I hope you can find some inspiration and motivation from my story. Even though I've messed up many times and I still may slip up now and then, I'm making progress. For a time, I had pretty much determined that I'd forever be a miserable person who took drugs and drank and blamed everybody else for my worthless life. But I've really come a long way from being that guy.

I WAS STUCK IN THE *I'M WORTHLESS AND I DON'T DESERVE ANYTHING BETTER* ZONE.

Although I didn't take that journey alone, my transformation had to begin with me. Nobody else could make that happen. There's no pill. No cocktail. No shot or powder. The first step is to decide that you want to be healthy, happy, trustworthy and deserving of love.

Being this new guy is more fun and more satisfying than I thought possible. I can't tell you how depressing and lonely it was to always be the disappointment. Every time I did something stupid or harmful, Kevin, A.J., Howie and Brian would hang their heads. I could see them fighting to control their anger and frustration with me. I felt the level of trust sink lower and lower.

I knew my behavior was unacceptable, self-destructive, and damaging to our relationship and our careers. I was still in the victim stage, still lying to myself, telling myself that I didn't have the power to change. I was stuck in the *I'm worthless and I don't deserve anything better* zone.

I'm not in that zone any more. I'm on the comeback trail, reunited with all of my fellow Backstreet Boys and, even better, I'm back on track to being the person I've wanted to be; someone worthy of their respect, trust and love.

PERSONAL NOTES

CHAPTER TEN

THE DAY-TO-DAY CHALLENGES & REWARDS

MY GRANDPA, DOUG Spaulding, my mother's father, was my biggest role model as a boy. I really looked up to him more and more after I became committed to bettering my life. Sadly, on January 4, 2013, as I was working on this very chapter, he passed away from emphysema at the age of 79.

As much as we may work day in and day out to do and be our best, we can't expect to be protected from other setbacks and losses. Hard times will still hit. The hope is that we get stronger as we go, and become better equipped to deal with the challenges that arise. I realized this even more after losing my grandfather, one of the most important figures in my life.

Grandpa Spaulding was a man of many talents. He was a high school English and drama teacher, a weekly newspaper editor, host and producer of two local television shows, and an avid reader. He had thousands of books in his home. I was in awe of his library and fascinated by his elegant, scholarly ways. He loved classical music and literature, especially the work of Shakespeare.

He studied literature his entire life. He was everything I wanted to be, including an actor. He had performed in college theatre and was fondest of his role as King Lear. He also wrote and directed plays and had worked on a couple video projects with his fellow Chautauqua, New York residents, Bill and Hillary Clinton.

My grandfather often talked about the time he took me to see *Hansel and Gretel* at the Chautauqua Opera when I was three years old. He said I was so enthralled I stood up through the entire performance. Grandpa believed that show was one of my inspirations to become a performer. There is also the story of him taking me to see a live performance of *The Wizard of Oz* when I was about five years old. I was so scared of the witch, I cried.

Grandpa's death was especially sad for me because he was the one truly thoughtful person I could call whenever I needed someone to talk to. I knew he cared about me. His love was unconditional. He would send me books to read, especially on holistic health therapies and medical breakthroughs, and we'd discuss all the things we'd learned from them.

I FEEL IT IS IMPORTANT TO HAVE SOMEONE TO LOOK UP TO...

Grandpa Spaulding was amazing because his interest in learning never diminished over the years. Even in his late seventies, he was constantly on the Internet looking up things on Google, always seeking new information. I respected his hunger for knowledge. He helped motivate me to keep learning and expanding my understanding of the world. He was so smart. Every time we visited or talked, I wanted to soak up as much from him as I could.

I feel it is important to have someone to look up to whether it's a respected friend, a parent or grandparent, or maybe even an older sibling. We can't choose which people cross our paths in life, but we can choose which ones to associate with and learn from. I encourage you to look for the kind of positive people who will inspire you and make you want to be the best at whatever you do.

My grandfather is the person who introduced me to a saying by Benjamin Franklin that has stayed with me: "If you lie down with dogs, you'll get up with fleas." In other words, the people you hang out with ultimately have an impact on you, so you should choose your friends and mentors wisely. Grandma Spaulding told me recently that my grandpa was my biggest fan, but little did he know I was *his* biggest fan. I will miss him. Before he died, I told him that I would make him proud and that I'd also make sure people remembered him. I want to live up to his example. I want to be as good a man as he was, and I want to serve as a role model for others, the way he served as mine.

THE REWARDS OF A BETTER LIFE

One of the cool things about trying to be as good as my Grandpa Spaulding is that I'm now feeling things I hadn't felt while binge drinking, doing drugs, popping pills, and partying every night.

For instance, the other day someone asked me the usual question, "How's it going Nick?"

"Great!" I said. "My life is going great."

And for the first time in many years, I meant it from my heart and soul.

How many times do we answer that sort of question on automatic pilot, saying what we think we ought to say but not feeling it? Well, I'm definitely feeling it like never before.

I've experienced what it's like to be in a depressing downward spiral where bad things just seem to mount until it feels like the weight of the world and maybe the entire universe is on your back. Now, I'm in a different kind of whirlwind, a positive upward sweep. I'm healthy and happy, and good things seem to keep coming my way.

NOW, I'M IN A DIFFERENT KIND OF WHIRLWIND, A POSITIVE UPWARD SWEEP.

I've noticed that people who used to avoid me when I was in the dumps are coming back around now. In my dark days, strangers offered me drugs or shots of booze. Now strangers offer me opportunities, book deals, movie deals, and record deals. I like these *dealers* better. There's more of a future for me in what they offer. There was no future in the other life I led.

Bad things still happen, of course. There are still conflicts and challenges to deal with each and every day, but now I'm in a much better position to overcome them and to find solutions that don't add to my problems. For many years, I played the victim—or just as bad, I played the blame game. But fortunately I'm out of those roles and games for good.

Now, I'm into forgiveness and gratitude. One of the things I've discovered in my efforts to build a better life is that alcohol and drugs weren't the worst poisons I was putting into my body. The anger, resentment, and bitterness that I harbored for my parents and a few others—even for myself sometimes—was toxic.

When you allow those negative emotions to dominate your thoughts and control your actions over long periods, they trigger stress, which releases chemicals in your body that can do every bit as much damage as alcohol and drugs. They compromise your immune system, raise your blood pressure, weaken your heart, and cause all sorts of other physical problems.

Maybe even worse, bottled up anger, bitterness and resentment toward just one person could poison *all* of your relationships. Those negative feelings are so volatile that they limit your ability to trust, empathize, and communicate effectively, even with those you love the most. When you assume the part of the victim, you tend to see everyone around you as a victimizer. When you play the blame game, you tend to dodge responsibility for your own actions and for your own happiness.

The cure for victimization and blame is forgiveness. I used to reject that idea because I didn't want to do any favors for people who'd hurt me. Then it was pointed out to me that you don't forgive people for their sake, you do it for yourself. Forgiveness frees you from anger, bitterness and resentment. It allows you to stop living in the past and clears the path for you to live for the future instead.

THE CURE FOR
VICTIMIZATION AND
BLAME IS FORGIVENESS.

At first, you may not be able to forgive someone who has done something terrible to you. That can be a big step. Instead, try a smaller one. Forgive someone who has hurt you just a little: Maybe the guy who stole your parking space at the mall? Or the co-worker who asked if you'd put on weight over the holidays? Start small and see what it feels like.

If the person you need to forgive isn't a loved one or a valued friend, you can look at it this way: forgiving that person makes him or her less important to you. A friend of mine describes these hurtful, but unimportant people as *scenery in my life*. They are there, but you don't have to pay much attention to them. You don't give them any power over you or your emotions.

Forgiving a loved one or a valued friend is trickier, but more important. I don't claim to be a master of this yet. I'm still working on it. Those loved ones have the power to hurt you the most because you care about them so much. For this reason, forgiving them may have to be done in stages. First you forgive them just for your own sake. You don't want what they did to have a lasting and far-reaching effect on your life. It's like disarming a bomb. If you don't take away its explosive power, you'll never know when it will go off or what damage it will wreak when it does erupt.

I DON'T TRY TO ERASE THE MEMORY OF THE BAD THINGS I'VE DONE.

As time passes and your ability to forgive grows and strengthens, you can work on forgiving loved ones or friends for their sakes too. No one is saying you have to forget what someone did to you, but having that person back in your life in a positive way could benefit you both.

Of course, forgiveness is also a gift you give yourself. I've had to work on acknowledging and accepting this truth, too. I've already told you that for a long time I didn't feel worthy of success as a performer. Well, I didn't feel worthy of forgiveness either. While you've read about many of my biggest mistakes and misjudgments there are still others in my past I haven't shared, and I'm sure there will be even more down the road.

With help, I've learned to be more forgiving of myself. I don't try to erase the memory of the bad things I've done. I want to learn from them and remember them so that I can avoid making the same mistakes again and again. I'm slowly getting better and granting myself forgiveness for each of these offenses, one at a time. I'm learning to see mistakes and failures as opportunities to learn and grow.

SHIFTING PERSPECTIVE

This brings us to the second powerful tool I've found. Gratitude has amazing powers because it can shift your entire perspective. An attitude of gratitude can take a negative, aggravating, and stressful experience and turn it into a meaningful and positive one.

Here's an example: We were recently working in the studio on our latest album when gratitude altered the entire event for me. I was feeling overwhelmed and run down. Recording an album has sometimes been likened to making sausage; it can be a bloody mess that's not much fun to watch even if the end result is awesome. You often have to sing entire songs and bits of songs over and over again just to get the right sound on tape. Then there are usually hours upon hours of trying different arrangements, adding this instrument, tweaking that chorus or deleting a solo. It can be mind-numbing waiting for it all to come together.

THAT'S THE MAGIC OF
GRATITUDE.

So, I was sitting there with my head down on the counter top, feeling exhausted, when the engineer finally played the song we'd been working on all night. It sounded amazing. In that very moment, I felt this tidal wave of gratitude. It hit me that I was really living the dream. Not just *my* dream, but also the dream of millions of other singers and performers. I was working on a record with some of the most talented production people in the world, surrounded by wonderful musicians and singers. What was boring or tedious or exhausting about that?

In an instant, I reframed the entire experience from something negative and draining to something very positive and empowering. That's the magic of gratitude. Another great thing about gratitude is that you can apply it even to the challenges in your life. You don't have to like it when you get fired or when you are turned down for a promotion. You won't be thrilled either when someone disappoints you or lies to you. But you can be grateful for the opportunities that come with every challenge. Maybe being fired or turned down for a promotion will lead to something bigger and better. Maybe being disappointed or lied to by someone will lead to your finding another person who is more supportive and reliable.

STEPPING STONES

In this final chapter, my goal is to help you see the power of forgiveness and gratitude when applied to your own life. When you use them on a daily basis, you will feel lighter, unburdened, and energized. The path to a better life is taken step by step, day by day. I've made this point through-out the book, but here it is one last time: You won't change lifelong patterns overnight. You especially don't cure alcohol or drug addiction easily. True addiction is a disease and you probably won't ever feel like you've been cured, but you can become skilled at managing it.

What you can do is take life and its challenges one day at a time. You do this by replacing the negative thoughts, the addictive cravings and bad impulses with more positive payoffs and activities. These days, when I feel frustrated or overloaded, I don't hit the bars. I hit the gym, the beach, or the studio. I work to replace the detrimental attitudes and habits that limited me or tore me down with new constructive versions that build me up and open the door to better experiences.

YOU WON'T CHANGE
LIFELONG PATTERNS
OVERNIGHT.

Yes, it's a daily struggle. And yes, it's worth it. Even the simple things seem better. As I mentioned earlier, I just started playing basketball again, and I don't think I've ever enjoyed the game more. I have loved the sport ever since I was very young, but when I was overweight, drinking and doing drugs, there was no joy in it for me. I pretty much quit playing. In that time, I forgot how much it meant to me.

Now I play with a group of street-ballers who share my love for the game. They are serious playground athletes with amazing talent. After a couple of hours on the court with them, I can hardly walk, but man the endorphins are flowing and as tired as I am, I feel like a million bucks. The strange thing is that all of that exercise energizes me, and when I wake up the next day, I feel good about myself. That never happened when I spent the previous day or night—or both—out partying. Back then, I'd always felt guilty, like I was wasting my life and destroying my mind and body, which, of course, I was.

I'm not saying that the craving for alcohol doesn't still hit me, but more and more I feel my body craving exercise and my hope is that one day, the good will replace the bad entirely. Something else I've noticed: When you feel healthier, more alert mentally, and more engaged in life, you seem to put some sort of aura or vibe out in the world that draws similar people to you.

WE NEED TO ENCOURAGE EACH OTHER, CHEER EACH OTHER ON, AND STEER EACH OTHER BACK ONTO THE POSITIVE PATH.

Honestly, I've had more friends and strangers tell me that I look awesome or that I'm singing great in the last few months than ever in my life. The guys in the group can't seem to stop telling me how cool it is to see me enjoying myself in the studio and on stage again. Their positive feedback makes me want to work even harder on bettering my career, my relationships and myself.

I've even had several people say things like, "You know, I was worried that you wouldn't be around much longer, that you'd be dead someday, and now I'm so happy that you've turned your life around." I wish they'd never had to think of me as someone who was self-defeating, but I'm very grateful to them for leveling with me, and for encouraging me.

We have to do that. We need to encourage each other, cheer each other on, and steer each other back onto the positive path. It's easy to get caught up in your own struggles and to miss the fact that the person beside you is struggling too, maybe even more than you are. So, once you've managed to pull yourself up and you are feeling better, make sure to reach out to others still trying to make it.

BETTER DAYS

Now that I'm seriously working on being a better person and building a better life, my mission is to never get too comfortable. I want to keep challenging myself, especially by doing things that mentally strengthen me and expand my horizons. Acting is one of the things I want to try again.

You may recall that in my darker days I blew an opportunity to work on my chops as an actor. I landed a role as a bully in the 2004 teen horror movie *The Hollow*, but instead of spending my nights nailing my lines and preparing for each day's shoot, I went out partying. My hung-over appearance and shaky performance may be the scariest things in that movie, which still shows up on the Syfy channel now and then.

I've felt badly for a long time about not giving my best effort on that set, but I've forgiven myself, and I am committed to reviving this dream. I've been interested in acting and making movies ever since I won that video camera as a kid competing on *The New Original Amateur Hour* television show in Orlando. Again, some of my best childhood memories are the home movies and skits I made with my brother and sisters. I've been involved in some film projects since then. For example, I directed one of my music videos and I've written some screenplays.

In 2012, I took my first serious step back toward acting by enrolling in a series of workshops by L.A. acting coach John Rosenfeld. John takes a very personal and therapeutic approach to the craft. He encourages his students to work on themselves as well as on their acting skills because he believes your personal growth helps you develop as an actor. He also says that the walls you run into in your acting are the same walls you run into in your personal life.

John is the perfect acting coach for me. He has helped me tear down some of those walls I've built around my emotions over the years. It's been a powerful experience. One of the problems that stifled my earlier acting attempts was the notion I've carried around for years that I'm horrible at memorization. A bad memory is a serious handicap when you have to learn your lines for a movie or television show.

This insecurity dates back to my grade-school days. I probably freaked out on some homework assignment to memorize the Gettysburg Address or a Yeats poem. I've lugged that self-limiting thought around with me my whole life. Even though I have memorized hundreds of songs over the years, I was still stuck in the belief that I didn't have a good enough memory to master my lines as an actor.

Basically, I put a label on myself identifying me as someone who didn't have what it takes to fulfill that particular dream, and then I lived down to that low expectation by showing up on the set with a hangover. That's messed up, right? I couldn't even tell you why I thought my memory sucked, but I let that self-limiting thought stay in my head all this time. Why didn't I just go with the fact that a professional casting director thought I could play the role in the movie? I didn't give myself the same credit that the casting director did.

I OFTEN WONDER WHY WE LET THOSE NEGATIVE THOUGHTS HAVE SUCH AN IMPACT.

My therapist tells me that I should never allow what happened to me in the past affect my future. That's exactly what I was doing. You might want to ask yourself if you've also put labels and limitations on yourself that keep you from claiming the life you want. Have you told yourself you're not smart enough, not talented enough, or not worthy of what you want? I often wonder why we let those negative thoughts have such an impact. Why don't we hold onto positive thoughts in the same way?

Instead of letting one minor memory failure as a kid stick with me for so long, why didn't I go with the fact that at the age of twelve, I was already so polished as a performer that my choices were to join the cast of Disney's *All New Mickey Mouse Club* show or the band Backstreet Boys? Why didn't

I apply some gratitude for my success as a singer and performer and use that to boost my confidence instead of feeling unworthy?

Those are questions that I'm asking myself in the acting workshop exercises I'm participating in now. Psychologically, it's very intense. John wants us to be in touch with our emotions. In the past, I often ran from mine. Usually, I tried to drown them in alcohol or numb them with drugs. But John has made me open up old wounds and look at them to determine what caused them and how each of them impacted the way I see and respond to the world around me.

I've learned that you have to allow yourself to be vulnerable in order to become stronger. It's tough. Like most people, I don't like reliving painful events or memories. I'm much more inclined to bury them or let them remain locked away. But I've learned that what is easier for us isn't necessarily what is better for us.

LETTING GO

Too often, when we're hurt we close up to protect ourselves. We don't express our feelings so they fester inside, causing confusion, frustration and anger. Guys are known for that, but women do it too. Another *guy thing* that I'm guilty of is holding back, which you can't do as an actor. Most of the other participants in John's workshop are younger than me, yet they are more experienced as actors. Many majored in theater in college. Some have already worked regularly in commercials, movies and television shows. They see me as this older, sort of uptight, pop star guy who has sold millions of albums but is somehow just raw as an actor. I feel pretty vulnerable and humble when I see how good most of the kids in my workshop are. They can cut loose and get into character much easier than I can.

John has had me working on that, to the point that it's a little scary and shocking. After the first few days in his class I found myself crying over things I never thought I'd cry over. For instance, I was home on my computer one night and I randomly clicked on a music video by the rock group Heart with the sisters Ann and Nancy Wilson. I love Nancy's guitar playing especially. But this time, something just came over me. I got all teary-eyed as I watched their performance and I couldn't figure out why. A friend told me later that the song must have "hit a cord with me"—reminding me of something in my past, something that triggered a strong, long-buried emotion.

I really don't know what memories came up with that Heart song, but I'm glad it happened. It's good to relieve those pent-up feelings. Crying provides a huge release of stress and pressure. I used to have a hard time crying, probably because my dad was a tough guy and he saw it as a sign of weakness. When I cried as a kid, he would smack me upside the head and tell me to stop being a baby.

I ENCOURAGE YOU TO LET THE TEARS SLIP WHENEVER THE INSTINCT STRIKES YOU.

More recently, I've learned that crying is a natural response to certain deeply felt emotions. We really shouldn't try to hold back our tears because keeping those feelings bottled up actually makes us more vulnerable. I usually feel much better after something causes me to cry, so I don't look at it as a bad thing anymore.

You shouldn't look at crying as a bad thing either. I encourage you to let the tears slip whenever the instinct strikes you. If it helps to open up with a friend or a therapist, then do that. John Rosenfeld's class provided me with the support and encouragement I needed to finally break through the barriers I'd built around my feelings since childhood. I find that every time I allow myself to open up and be vulnerable, I learn something new about myself, and I feel stronger.

John wants his students to be as free as children playing in his workshops. His classes are forcing me to let go of the things that have held me back in my acting. It's all about recapturing that childhood joy, enthusiasm and fearlessness. I've been able to tap into the feelings I had in the early days of BSB when we had so much fun dancing and singing onstage, and just enjoying all of the opportunities that came our way.

I want to bring that joyful attitude now into every aspect of my life.

I believe that my experience in John's workshop will make me a better all-around person and performer. I'm more aware of my feelings, more conscious of how things affect me, more focused on the positive, and I'm feeling much more optimistic about my future.

LASTING BONDS

When you live on the edge as long as I did, you can't possibly foresee all of the rewards that come with a healthier, saner, and more sober lifestyle. This is especially true for me in my interactions with other people. I've had very few *normal* relationships in my life.

You've already learned more about my family dysfunction than you've probably ever wanted to know. And my experiences with girlfriends haven't been the most stable either. Even the relationships that didn't make the tabloids were pretty tumultuous. Most of them didn't last very long either.

Part of the problem was my globetrotting lifestyle, of course. Sure, it can be a glamorous and fun. We had a ball in the early years. But for every song written about the good ole wild and crazy times on the road, there is another one or two about the loneliness, monotony and disconnection that comes with constantly moving from one venue and hotel room to the next.

I'm grateful for the opportunities, of course. I wouldn't trade my experiences for anything. There's no other job that would have allowed a working class kid from Tampa to see so much of the world, or to make such a great living. Still, I often found myself envying people who had more balanced lives and long-term, loving and supportive relationships.

I WOULDN'T TRADE MY EXPERIENCES FOR ANYTHING.

Girls came and went with me. I could never hold on to a relationship. I didn't trust anybody and because I was immature and a control freak, I often saw the girls I dated as controlling. I'd break up, saying I didn't want another person telling me what to do or putting demands on me.

When you are in a committed relationship, you are accountable to the other person. You have to consider the impact that your actions and words have on your partner. Back then I couldn't handle being responsible and considerate of another person all the time.

I was more about drinking and partying and hanging out with my friends. I was locked into that 19-year-old-guy mindset, and most of the people I hung out with shared my views. I was surrounded by self-centered people who were all about getting drunk and stoned. It was a negative environment. We were the misery-loves-company crowd. Our relationships were built on nothing more than our shared lack of responsibility. We weren't really friends at all. We were mostly just enablers for each other's worst habits.

My life has changed so much for the better in that regard too. What may be the greatest reward, and the most telling sign that I am recovering from my past mistakes, is the fact that I've been in a healthy, loving relationship with a wonderful woman named Lauren Kitt for the past four years—the longest relationship of my life. I'm extraordinarily happy. We have been doing really well in the last few years especially, and it's because I'm learning to be a better person and a better partner in the relationship.

I've come a long way in that regard. My focus has had to change. Lauren has taught me a lot. She is intelligent, a genuine and honest person, and she is my best friend. I've just never had anyone I could totally trust like Lauren. Having a stable relationship with her has made such a difference.

MY FOCUS HAS HAD
TO CHANGE.

We've both had our challenges with alcohol, drugs and weight, so we understand each other and support each other mentally and spiritually. We both want to be healthier in mind and body. Fitness is common ground for us. We motivate each other and use sports as a way to combat depression and release healthy endorphins. Lauren has been a rock for me, the person I can go to and feel normal with. We play tennis and video games and we work out together. We do weightlifting and cardio conditioning, too. We've even played paintball together. She once shot me point blank, which was not fun. It stung like hell and left a mark. She's got mad skills as an athlete, that's for sure.

Lauren is a model and professional bodybuilder who has earned her pro card with the World Bodybuilding and Fitness Federation (WBFF) in Dallas. She is athletic and super-competitive, which keeps things interesting because we push each other to be better all the time. And we've enjoyed motivating other people as well; we started a YouTube TV show and website together called *Kitt Fit* that focuses on the fitness portion of our lives. We really are very dedicated to showing others how to stay active and healthy. I particularly like that we have grown as people as we've grown together. We've become more than either of us ever thought we could be.

I've had relationships that didn't seem to go anywhere beyond the initial physical attraction. Some of the women I've dated actually made me feel worse about myself. A few were just fans curious about the celebrity life or they were looking to help their careers by hanging out with me.

I ENJOY LEARNING HOW TO BE A
MORE THOUGHTFUL
AND CARING PERSON.

My connection with Lauren is healthier than any I've had because it is based on our shared desire to be better and to live more meaningful lives. Together, we feel we can do anything we put our minds to. This sort of positive, empowering bond was the major missing piece in my life. Most of my previous relationships were superficial or unbalanced on one side or the other. There wasn't the same mutual respect and caring as I'm fortunate to experience now with Lauren. In the past, if I had a disagreement with a girlfriend it was often as if someone had lit a fuse. Explosives would go off. There was no search for understanding or solutions.

I'd become jaded. I'd given up on ever finding a person to share my life with. In a lot of ways I didn't know what constituted good or bad, right or wrong in this arena. I've had to study how my friends with solid relationships treat their wives and how they respond to each other. I try to apply the lessons I've learned to my own life. These observations have helped make me an infinitely better partner. It's exciting, really. I enjoy learning how to be a more thoughtful and caring person. I don't always succeed. Most men have a lot to learn when it comes to communicating with women. But I continue to try and the results of those efforts are rewarding.

Lauren isn't afraid to give me a reality check now and then, but even when she does, we can usually just talk through things without blowing up. Taking alcohol and drugs out of the equation definitely helps. We're not going out partying every night. I spent so much of my life in bars and clubs, wasting time that I should've spent in acting classes or writing songs—making improvements that would have put me ahead of the game. I'm making up for lost time now, and having this stable relationship has been a major factor.

Whenever I'm feeling sad or depressed about Leslie's death, my poor relationship with my parents or other personal issues, Lauren is there for me. She is so understanding. She'll comfort me and give me time to be sad or to vent, all while encouraging me to be forgiving toward others and myself too. She gives me room to deal with my demons in a sane and healthy way.

BEING THERE FOR EACH OTHER

Other girls in my life would often criticize me for my feelings, take the other side—or worse, they just wouldn't want to deal with me when I wasn't fun to be around. Lauren never says that I shouldn't feel one way or another, or that I'm wrong. She says, "I love you and I don't want you to hurt yourself. It pains me when you are hurting and self-destructive because I want us to be together for a long time. I love you. I want you to be here."

We've talked about the way my sister died from an overdose, whether intentional or accidental, and Lauren is clear about needing me and wanting us to live long lives together. We're sometimes a little extreme in our focus on fitness, but even when we're over the top, at least it's a healthy fixation. If either one of us has a checkup and our blood pressure is up or we've gained weight, we're all over it, correcting the problem quickly because we want to wake up every morning to see each other's face. We want to be there for each other.

That's such a shift for me. I've clearly moved away from being focused on my problems and needs and am now moving toward having a more balanced outlook in life and love. I guess it is part of an evolving and more grown-up perspective. I've learned with Lauren that you can't change other people, but that's the wrong goal anyway. If you truly care about someone and want to build a lasting relationship with them, you work on yourself first and serve as an example.

WE WANT TO BE THERE FOR EACH OTHER.

There may be things about your partner that you don't like, but if you look within yourself, you'll likely find a lack of perfection there too. You should never accept abusive behavior, of course. Sometimes we do fall for people who aren't right for us. In that instance, you have to be able to see the relationship for what it is and make the decision to walk away. I've made that decision before and know it can be painful, even when it's apparent that it's the right thing to do. Remember that when you walk away from a bad relationship, you're actually taking one step closer to finding a better relationship. One that's truly right for you.

With Lauren, I want to be a better person, which tells me that she is good for me. We make each other want to strive to be our best selves. The point I want to make in this last chapter is that if you aren't finding long-term relationships that make you want to be a better partner and person, maybe the problem isn't the people you are dating. Maybe the problem lies somewhere within you.

That was my case, for the most part. I wasn't satisfied with anyone else primarily because I wasn't satisfied with myself. My relationship with Lauren didn't really take root until I became committed to having a healthier, saner, and more positive life. Lauren bought into that person and now we inspire each other to fulfill that dream for ourselves and for each other.

SEEKING TO UNDERSTAND

We've both done self-destructive things in the past. However, now that we've built something really beautiful together, we realize that we'd have so much more to lose if we ever jeopardized it. That knowledge gives us greater incentive to preserve and cultivate what we have. We've identified not only the sort of people we want to be, but the kind of relationship we want to enjoy together. Our physical attraction is strong. Being friends to each other is equally important. Sometimes that means giving each other a friendly kick in the butt, or a wake-up call, or another point of view. Love is not just about smiling and being agreeable.

If relationships were an extreme sport, my family would have been Olympians in that category. When things were good, we were all hugs and kisses and "I love you, too." When things were bad, we'd shriek, throw things at each other, and punch and scream for hours. There was very little middle ground. Lauren and I don't want that.

IF RELATIONSHIPS WERE AN EXTREME SPORT, MY FAMILY WOULD HAVE BEEN OLYMPIANS IN THAT CATEGORY.

We don't mind being a boring couple now and then. Boring has its good points. We try not to let small things blow up into big problems. Before meeting Lauren, I had a tendency to sulk and keep my feelings locked up until the pressure built so much that I'd explode. I avoided conflict because in my childhood, there was no such thing as a gentle disagreement. My father let off steam by shooting a gun out the window. Can you imagine the fear that created in our household?

Lauren is a strong woman, physically and emotionally, but I don't ever want her to fear me in that way. So, building a relationship is just as much about knowing what you don't want, as knowing what you do want. That's all part of it. I'm learning to take responsibility for how I make her feel, which is a big step for me and for most guys.

Women often assume we understand their feelings, but most men aren't wired like that. So when we are committed to someone who matters to us, we are sometimes slow to grasp that women don't want us to *fix* their situations as much as they want us to understand how they feel about them.

I don't pretend to have the male-female dynamics all figured out yet. At one time in my life, I feared I'd never have a girlfriend for more than a few years.

And even if I did, I feared marriage. (Don't even get me started on my fear of kids!) But I am maturing and my outlook on many things is changing.

When I first met Lauren, I told her that I never wanted to get married. My parents' *union* had served as such a bad example, I just didn't believe in it. I wanted her to hear it from me firsthand. But when you grow to truly love someone, you feel very protective of that person. Especially when that person is as dedicated to you as Lauren is to me—when that person is by your side everyday supporting your needs and goals. You see in their actions that they have committed their life to you. And because their life has value, too, you have to be fair. You can't just play with another person's life. You're either in or you're out. Before I knew it, I was dedicated to Lauren, too.

WHEREAS THE THOUGHT OF BEING COMMITTED TO ONE PERSON FOR SO LONG WAS ONCE SCARY TO ME, I ACTUALLY FIND IT LIBERATING NOW.

Whereas the thought of being committed to one person for so long was once scary to me, I actually find it liberating now. I am much freer to be myself when I'm with Lauren because she and I know and trust each other so much. That sense of freedom is something I never expected in a relationship, but I'm really grateful for it.

Today, I'm happy to say that not only can I *imagine* spending a lifetime with Lauren, I'm really *looking forward* to it. In February of 2013, I proposed to her in one of my favorite places on earth and she said, "Yes!" We had planned a 10-day vacation in the Florida Keys. I bought the ring in advance, and by the time we got down there I had wanted to finally give it to her. I felt like it was burning a hole in my pocket for a while already. The plan was to take a 25-foot boat I kept down there to a private island that is very special to me. I chose that location because I wanted Lauren to visit a place from my childhood that held happy memories, especially since she had mostly heard about all the bad things from that time in my life.

Although I loved fishing and boating, I hadn't been to the Keys in more than 8 years. What I didn't realize before we arrived was that after all that time being docked in the marina, the boat would be in such bad condition.

I knew I just couldn't let anything disrupt my plans, so Lauren's father and I spent three whole days taking that boat apart and restoring it as best we could. We ripped the engine out and replaced all the gunked-up parts until it was functioning enough to take out for a ride. On that day, we almost didn't make it to the island. We got to a sand mound and the engine stopped. I had to restart it several times, but it was really touch and go. Can you imagine if we got stuck out there? It's so remote we would have had to call the Coast Guard. It was an adventure, but we finally got to where I intended to go. We call it *Engagement Island* because where it's located is still a secret and we want to keep it that way. That's where I finally popped the question and Lauren happily agreed to spend the rest of her life with me.

In so many ways that trip is a metaphor for the long and determined journey I've described for you in this book. I've had to take my life apart, examine it, figure out what needed fixing and make the necessary changes to get me where I so badly wanted to be, just as I had to do with that boat. One of the many wonderful things about returning to Florida on that trip was that I got a chance to stare down some of the worst demons of my past and prove to myself that I am stronger than I've ever been. It was such a mind-cleansing and healing experience and I'm so grateful for it. I am confident now that I can continue to grow and be the man I want to be for my own sake and the sake of my future wife. I'm excited by what both the present and the future hold for us.

I don't have any further thoughts about kids at the moment, but I'll say this much: As my married friends who served as such good relationship role models have and raise kids, I'll be watching and learning from those relationships, too. If these friends are as good at parenting as I suspect they will be, then we might just consider it. Who knows? One thing I've learned from my experiences is that anything is possible, but I continue to take life one step at a time as that has been a very good approach for me.

WRITING MY OWN STORY

Every day I'm learning more about myself and my ability to create my own life story. I'm feeling better about my future thanks to my more positive outlook and lifestyle, my reunion with Backstreet Boys, my renewed interest in songwriting and acting, my solid and loving relationship with Lauren and, of course, our impending marriage. Every day is a new day, and I never know what will be thrown at me, but now I'm confident that I have the power to handle life's challenges and the grace to appreciate its many gifts.

I know, too, that I can change myself for the better as long as I'm healthy in my mind and my body. I want to build on the good things in my life and I want to put the bad things in my rear view mirror, leaving them far behind forever. I do still deal with depression, which may be due to the drugs I've done in the past or, more generally, to my unhealthy former lifestyle. But I've learned to manage those moments, rather than allowing them to overwhelm me and trigger self-destructive behavior.

I COACH MYSELF TO SNAP OUT OF IT.

Being aware of negative thoughts and countering them immediately has been a big help. I coach myself to snap out of it. I use them as motivation to find something positive to do—anything that steers me away from darkness and toward the light.

We have an incredible ability to adjust our actions and thoughts. If we consistently monitor our feelings and make the necessary adjustments, the process gets easier and easier over time. My addictive craving now is to be healthy mentally, physically, and emotionally. I'm reading to open and expand my mind. I'm working out to strengthen my body. I'm in therapy to deal with my demons, manage my emotions, and just to be an all-around better person.

This book is one result of that commitment. I've tried to make it clear throughout these pages that I don't see myself as wiser or more evolved than anyone else. It's quite the opposite. The more I learn, the more humble

I feel because there is so much more out there beyond my grasp. As I stated in the introduction, I hope you learn from my mistakes. I've shared so many of them with you and must admit that reliving them wasn't easy.

THE MORE I LEARN, THE MORE HUMBLE I FEEL...

The other main point I hope you will take away from this book is that no matter how deep you may fall into that dark pit of despair, no matter how many mistakes you make, or how many failures you may experience, you can always turn your life around. You can be the person you want to be, the person you were meant to be. Don't ever give up on yourself. Don't ever let anyone else write your story for you. Write your own. Know that you are worthy of the best life you can create.

Reading this book is one step in that turnaround process. I encourage you to keep going, step by step, day by day. You may stumble, fall down, or screw up. I certainly have. You will find, though, that when you keep getting up and working for the life you want, you get better and better at being better and better. Just vow to learn from those mistakes and to forgive yourself. Vow to do your best. If you maintain that commitment and a positive attitude, I believe good things will happen for you just as they have for me. You have nothing to lose by trying and believe me the rewards are sweet!

DON'T EVER LET ANYONE ELSE WRITE YOUR STORY FOR YOU.

PERSONAL NOTES

DISCOGRAPHY & AWARDS

BACKSTREET BOYS

1996 – *Backstreet Boys*
1997 – *Backstreet's Back*
1999 – *Millennium*
2000 – *Black & Blue*
2005 – *Never Gone*
2007 – *Unbreakable*
2009 – *This Is Us*
2013 – *In a World Like This*

SOLO

2002 – *Now or Never*
2011 – *I'm Taking Off*

AWARDS

1995   Smash Hits – Best New Tour Act

1996   Bravo Otto – Gold Pop Group
Goldene Kamera – Best Boy Band
MTV Europe Music Awards – MTV Select: "Get Down (You're the One for Me)"
Viva Comet Awards – Durchstarter (Best Newcomers) and the Shooting Star of the Year

1997   Bravo Otto – Gold Pop Group
MTV Europe Music Awards – Select: "As Long As You Love Me"
Viva Comet Awards – Durchstarter (Best Newcomers)
Diamond Award (Canada) – *Backstreet Boys* certified as a Diamond
    album in Canada (1,000,000 units sold)

1998   Billboard Music Awards – Group Album of the Year: *Backstreet Boys*
Bravo Otto – Gold Pop Group
ECHO Awards – Best International Group
MuchMusic Video Awards – People's Choice Favorite
    International Group
MTV Video Music Awards – Best Group Video: "Everybody
    (Backstreet's Back)"
Smash Hits Poll Winners Awards – Best Non-British Act
TMF Awards (Netherlands) –
    Best international album: *Backstreet Boys*
    Best international single: "As Long as You Love Me"
    Best international live act
Viva Comet Awards – Durchstarter (Best Newcomers)
World Music Awards – World's Best-selling Dance Artist
Diamond Award (Canada) – *Backstreet's Back* certified as
    a Diamond album in Canada (1,000,000 units sold)

1999   American Music Awards – Favorite Pop/Rock Band, Duo or Group
Grammy Awards – Best New Artist (nominated)
Billboard Music Awards –
    Album of the Year: *Millennium*
    Albums Artist Duo/Group of the Year
    Albums Artist of the Year
    Artist of the Year
Blockbuster Entertainment Awards –
    Favorite CD: *Millennium*
    Favorite Group: Pop
Bravo Otto – Silver Band
MuchMusic Video Awards – People's Choice Favorite
    International Group
MTV Europe Music Awards – Best Group
MTV Video Music Awards – Viewer's Choice: "I Want It That Way"
Nickelodeon Kids Choice Awards – Favorite Song: "Everybody
    (Backstreet's Back)"
Smash Hits Poll Winners Awards –

Best Band on Planet Pop
Best Non-British Band
Best Single of 1999: "I Want It That Way"
Best Album of 1999: *Millennium*
Best Pop Video: "Larger than Life"
Teen Choice Awards – Choice Music Video of the Year: "All I Have To Give"
Viva Comet Awards – Zuschauer-Comet Viva (Viewer's Choice)
World Music Awards – World's Best-selling Pop Group
Diamond Award (U.S.) –
Backstreet Boys certified as a Diamond album in the U.S. (10,000,000 units sold)
Millennium certified as a Diamond album in the U.S. (10,000,000 units sold)
Diamond Awards (Canada) – *Millennium* certified as a Diamond album in Canada (1,000,000 units sold)

2000   American Music Awards – Favorite Pop/Rock Band, Duo or Group
Grammy Awards –
Album of the Year: *Millennium* (nominated)
Best Pop Album: *Millennium* (nominated)
Record of the Year: "I Want It That Way" (nominated)
Best Pop Performance by a Duo or Group: "I Want It That Way" (nominated)
Bravo Otto – Gold Pop Group
Juno Award – Best-selling Album (foreign or domestic): *Millennium*
Nickelodeon Kids Choice Awards – Favorite Music Group
MTV Europe Music Awards – Best Group
People's Choice Awards – Favorite Musical Group
Teen Choice Awards – Choice Album: *Millennium*
World Music Awards –
World's Best-selling American Group
World's Best-selling Pop Group
World's Best-selling R&B Group
World's Best-selling Dance Artist
Radio Music Awards – Radio Slow Dance Song of the Year: "Show Me the Meaning of Being Lonely"

2001   American Music Awards – Favorite Pop/Rock Band, Duo or Group
Grammy Awards – Best Pop Performance by a Duo or Group with Vocal: "Show Me the Meaning of Being Lonely" (nominated)

MuchMusic Video Awards – People's Choice Favorite
   International Group
TMF Awards (Netherlands) – Best International Pop Group
World Music Awards –
      World's Best-selling Pop Group
      World's Best-selling American Group

2002   Grammy Awards – Best Pop Performance by a Duo or Group
      with Vocal: "Shape of My Heart" (nominated)
RIAJ – 17th Japan Gold Disc Award
MTV Video Music Awards Japan – Best Group
MTV Asia Awards – Favorite Video: "The Call"

2005   Bravo Otto – Bronze Pop Group

2006   MTV Asia Awards – Favorite Pop Act

2009   Starshine Music Awards – Best Live Show

2010   Japan Gold Disc Award – International Song of the Year:
      "Straight Through My Heart"
Starshine Music Awards –
      Best Dance Song: "Straight Through My Heart"
      Best Pop Song: "Bigger"
      Favorite Band/Group
      Best Live Show
      Song of the Year: "Straight Through My Heart"
      Album of the Year: *This Is Us*
      Artist of the Year

2011   NewNowNext Awards – Best New Indulgence: New Kids On The
      Block/Backstreet Boys – Summer Tour 2011

2013   Hollywood Walk of Fame – Star on the Walk of Fame

NOTE FROM LAUREN

Throughout our relationship, Nick has inspired and motivated me. His resilience and energy towards life are just a couple of his many admirable qualities that continue to transpire. I would not be the woman I am today if not for him and his unconditional love. I am immensely proud of him and all that he has accomplished and cannot wait to be one as husband and wife.

I will be there always to love, protect and support you. I love you, Boose.

Lauren Kitt

ACKNOWLEDGEMENTS

I WISH TO thank my grandfather, Douglas Spaulding, whose wisdom was such a great source of inspiration for me throughout my life. He was an amazing and accomplished man whose quest for knowledge and constant self-improvement was reflected in his extensive library. I remember cleaning his study as a child and being awed and fascinated by all of the books he had. I truly wish he could have read this one. Though he didn't live to see it published, I'm proud to add it to the world's library in his honor.

I also want thank the love of my life, my rock and stronghold, Lauren Kitt, who has seen me through many transformations and has urged me to accomplish more of my personal goals than I ever thought possible. She has had the faith, perseverance, and patience to stand by me as I learned a lifetime of valuable lessons in just a few intense years. Like so many other child celebrities, I stayed young in all the wrong ways for too many years and had a lot of growing up to do. Lauren was there for me as I made my way from being a boy to a man. I'm forever grateful to her for that and for all of her love.

Much appreciation goes to Lori Graf as well. She has served as a surrogate mother, as someone I could always talk to in times of need, and as someone I continue to look to up to with respect and admiration. She is one of life's genuine role models and I am fortunate to have her in my life.

I must also acknowledge each and every one of my bandmates. They have instilled values in me that I will hold for life; they have been with me through thick and thin and have served as an alternate family, often showing me other perspectives of what family is and can potentially be. They were "instrumental" in my evolution. In so many ways, they have helped me be who I am today. I love them like brothers.

Of course, I send a big shout-out to my amazing and loyal fans. You have shown me unconditional love for the past 20 years, sticking with me when I was up and when I was down. We've shared some real heart-ache—the kind I sing about, the kind we all experience from time to time, and the kind that caused me to almost self-destruct, but we've shared lots of good times, too. I want to thank you for believing in me and not giving up hope when I was going through those hard times. I know it wasn't easy to watch me grow up right before your eyes.

Many thanks as well to Jack Ketsoyan of EMC Bowery, Jay McGraw, Scott Waterbury and Lisa Clark of Bird Street Books, and to Wes Smith and Hope Innelli for helping me bring this book to the world. It's been a great journey.

BIBLIOGRAPHY

CHAPTER ONE

Everett, Cristina and Joyce Chen. "Nick and Aaron Carter's sister Leslie died from drug overdose, was under the influence of several prescription drugs: police report." *New York Daily News*. February 2, 2012. Accessed May 7, 2013. http://www.nydailynews.com/entertainment/gossip/nick-aaron-carter-sister-leslie-death-caused-prescription-drugs-addiction-article-1.1015933.

CHAPTER FOUR

"Drug Facts: MDMA (Ecstasy)." National Institute on Drug Abuse. Last modified December 2012. http://www.drugabuse.gov/publications/drugfacts/mdma-ecstasy.

"MDMA (Ecstasy) Abuse: What are the effects of MDMA?" National Institute on Drug Abuse. Last modified March 2006. http://www.drugabuse.gov/publications/research-reports/mdma-ecstasy-abuse/what-are-effects-mdma.

Fisk, John E., Philip N. Murphy, Catharine Montgomery, Florentia Hadjiefthyvoulou. "Modelling the adverse effects associated with ecstasy use." *Addiction*. 106. no. 4 (2011): 798-805. DOI: 10.1111/j.1360-0443.2010.03272.x (accessed April 26, 2013).

Di Iorio, Christina R., Tristan J. Watkins, Mary S. Dietrich, et al. "Evidence for Chronically Altered Serotonin Function in the Cerebral Cortex of Female 3,4-Methylenedioxymethamphetamine Polydrug Users." *Arch Gen Psychiatry.* 69. no. 4 (2012): 399-409. DOI:10.1001/archgenpsychiatry.2011.156 (accessed April 26, 2013).

Froelich, Paula. "Backstreet Boozer Busted for Brawl." *New York Post.* January 4, 2002. Accessed May 7, 2013. http://www.nypost.com/p/news/item_0qB15cxXULL3pIC61INc2M.

CHAPTER FIVE

Substance Abuse and Mental Health Services Administration. "Results from the 2011 National Survey on Drug Use and Health: Summary of National Findings." *NSDUH* Series H-44, HHS Publication No. (SMA) 12-4713. Rockville, MD: Substance Abuse and Mental Health Services Administration, 2012.

"1 in 4 High School Students and Young Adults Report Binge Drinking." Centers for Disease Control and Prevention. Last modified October 5, 2010. http://www.cdc.gov/media/pressrel/2010/r101005.html.

Centers for Disease Control and Prevention. "Vital Signs: Binge Drinking Prevalence, Frequency, and Intensity Among Adults – United States, 2010." *Morbidity and Mortality Weekly Report (MMWR).*61. no. 01 (2012): 14-19. http://www.cdc.gov/mmwr/preview/mmwrhtml/mm6101a4.htm?s_cid=mm6101a4_w (last modified January 13, 2012).

Naimi, TS, Brewer RD, Mokdad A, Denny C, Serdule MK, Marks JS. "Binge drinking among US adults." *JAMA.* 289. no. 1 (2003): 70-5. http://www.ncbi.nlm.nih.gov/pubmed/12503979?dopt=Abstract (accessed April 26, 2013).

"Fact Sheets – Underage Drinking." Centers for Disease Control and Prevention. Last modified October 29, 2012. http://www.cdc.gov/alcohol/fact-sheets/underage-drinking.htm.

"Teens and Young Adults Who Binge Drink Risk Negative Brain Effects Later in Life." *Huffington Post.* February 1, 2013. Accessed April 26, 2013. http://www.huffingtonpost.com/2013/02/01/binge-drink-brain-alcohol-young-adults-teens_n_2593315.html.

"Binge Drinking May Impair Teen Brain Development." *US News Health.* July 15, 2011. Accessed April 26, 2013. http://health.usnews.com/health-news/family-health/brain-and-behavior/articles/2011/07/15/binge-drinking-may-impair-teen-brain-development.

Baker, Al and Lisa W. Foderaro. "Tests Show Driver Was Drunk in Parkway Crash That Killed 8." *The New York Times.* August 4, 2009. Accessed April 26, 2013. http://www.nytimes.com/2009/08/05/nyregion/05crash.html?ref=dianeschuler&_r=1&.

Doward, Jamie. "Warning of extra heart dangers from mixing cocaine and alcohol." *The Guardian,* November 7, 2009. http://www.guardian.co.uk/society/2009/nov/08/cocaine-alcohol-mixture-health-risks.

"Results from the 2009 National Survey on Drug Use and Health: Volume I. Summary of National Findings." U.S. Department of Health and Human Services: Substance Abuse and Mental Health Services Administrations Office of Applied Studies. http://www.gmhc.org/files/editor/file/a_pa_nat_drug_use_survey.pdf.

"Mixing Alcohol with Other Drugs and/or Medications." Santa Clarita University. http://www.scu.edu/wellness/topics/alcohol/mixingalcohol.cfm.

"Drug Facts: Cocaine." National Institute on Drug Abuse. Revised April 2013. http://www.drugabuse.gov/publications/drugfacts/cocaine.

"Harmful Interactions: Mixing Alcohol with Medicines." National Institute on Alcohol Abuse and Alcoholism. http://pubs.niaaa.nih.gov/publications/Medicine/medicine.htm.

"Alcohol and Medication Interactions." WebMD. http://www.webmd.com/a-to-z-guides/alcohol-interactions-with-medications.

CHAPTER SEVEN

Huff, Richard. "No Need for Anyone to Get 'Carters'." *New York Daily News.* October 2, 2006. Accessed May 7, 2013. http://www.nydailynews.com/archives/entertainment/carters-article-1.646106.

CHAPTER EIGHT

"US drinks the lowest amount of alcohol in the developed world, figure reveal." *UK Daily News*, February 17, 2011. http://www.dailymail.co.uk/news/article-1357892/U-S-drinks-lowest-alcohol-developed-world-figures-reveal.html.

White, Megan. "Alcoholism in Russia." *Georgia Political Review*, February 6, 2012. Accessed on April 25, 2013. http://www.georgiapoliticalreview.com/alcoholism-in-russia/.

"Global Status Report on Alcohol and Health 2011." Word Health Organization. http://www.who.int/substance_abuse/publications/global_alcohol_report/en/index.html.

Office of Population Affairs. *Maturation of the Prefrontal Cortex.* http://www.hhs.gov/opa/familylife/tech_assistance/etraining/adolescent_brain/Development/prefrontal_cortex/.

RESOURCES

ALCOHOL / SUBSTANCE ABUSE RESOURCES

Alcoholics Anonymous
(212) 870-3400
www.aa.org

D.A.R.E.
(800) 223-DARE (3273)
www.dare.com/home/default.asp

Mothers Against Drunk Driving (MADD)
(877) ASK-MADD (275-6233)
www.madd.org

Partnership for a Drug-Free America
(855) 378-4373
www.drugfree.org

American Lung Association
(800) LUNGUSA (586-4872)
www.lung.org

National Clearinghouse for Alcohol and Drug Information
(800) 729-6686
www.ncadi.samhsa.gov

National Institute on Drug Abuse (NIDA)
(800) 662-HELP (4357)
www.drugabuse.gov

NIDA for Teens
www.teens.drugabuse.gov

National Association for Children of Alcoholics
(301) 468-0985
www.nacoa.org

Mental Help Net
www.mentalhelp.net

Recovery Happens Counseling Services
(916) 276-0626
www.recoveryhappens.com

Adult Children of Alcoholics
(310) 534-1815
www.adultchildren.org

National Council on Alcoholism and Drug Dependence, Inc. (NCADD)
(800) 622-2255
www.ncadd.org

Al-Anon and Al-ateen
(757) 563-1600
www.al-anon.alateen.org/

DOMESTIC VIOLENCE RESOURCES

National Domestic Violence Hotline:
(800) 799-SAFE (7233)
or 800.787.3224 (TTY)
www.thehotline.org

National Network to End Domestic Violence
(202) 543-5566
www.nnedv.org

American Psychiatric Association (APA)
(888) 35-PSYCH (77924)
www.healthyminds.org

National Coalition Against Domestic Violence
Phone: (800) 799-SAFE (7233)
Phone: (800) 787-3224 (TTY)
www.ncadv.org

The National Center for Victims of Crime
(202) 467-8700
www.victimsofcrime.org

National Resource Center on Domestic Violence
(800) 537-2238
www.nrcdv.org

National Center on Domestic Violence, Trauma & Mental Health
(312) 726-7020
 http://www.nationalcenterdvtraumamh.org/

National Teen Dating Abuse Helpline
(866) 331-9474
(866) 331-8453 (TTY)
www.loveisrespect.org

Safe Place
(512) 267-SAFE (7233)
www.safeplace.org

Health Resource Center on Domestic Violence
Phone: (800) 313-1310
Fax: (415) 252-8991

ANGER MANAGEMENT RESOURCES

National Anger Management Association (NAMA)
(646) 485-5116
namass@namass.org
namass.org

The Substance Abuse and Mental Health Services

www.samhsa.gov

SAMHSA Treatment Referral Helpline:

1-800-662-HELP (4357)

PERSONAL NOTES

PERSONAL NOTES